THE CONSUMER ADVOCATE'S GUIDE TO
HOME
INSPECTION

Avoiding the Nightmare of Purchasing a Money Pit

Barry Stone

Dearborn™
Trade Publishing
A **Kaplan Professional** Company

Vice President and Publisher: Cynthia A. Zigmund
Editorial Director: Donald J. Hull
Acquisitions Editor: Mary B. Good
Senior Project Editor: Jack Kiburz
Interior Design: Lucy Jenkins
Cover Design: DePinto Designs
Typesetting: Elizabeth Pitts

Published by Dearborn Trade Publishing
A Kaplan Professional Company

Printed in the United States of America

03 04 05 10 9 8 7 6 5 4 3 2 1

Library of Congress Cataloging-in-Publication Data

Stone, Barry.
   The consumer advocate's guide to home inspection : avoiding the nightmare of purchasing a money pit / Barry Stone.
     p.   cm.
Includes index.
   ISBN 0-7931-6032-4 (6 × 9 paperback)
   1. Dwellings—Inspection. 2. House buying. 3. Consumer protection.
I. Title.
   TH4817.5 .S76 2003
   643'.12—dc21

                      2002012127

DEDICATION

With gratitude and appreciation:
To my parents,
for unconditional love and a solid foundation;
To my wife, daughters, and son,
for giving life purpose and meaning;
To my friend and agent, Marc Davison,
for making this book possible;
And above all, to the Creator and Sustainer,
for all that is good and true.

ACKNOWLEDGMENTS

No one who assembles words, visions, and ideas for publication can ever say, "Alas, I did it alone!" All must humbly admit, to themselves and to the world at large, that other minds and hands were at work in the construction; that outside contributions of information, materials, logistics, encouragement, criticism, empathy, and more were as essential to the final outcome as were the creative efforts, sweat, and needless worry of the primary author. In recognition of this providential truth, I therefore submit the following expressions of sincere appreciation:

To my loyal wife, Ilona: Thanks for staying the course through years of efforts that have not always been fun or easy. In the hardest of times, you never gave up.

To my daughters, Dori and Janine, and to my son, Matt: You put up with the many nights and weekends when Dad was sequestered and unavailable, consumed with the writing of his book, when all you wanted was some time and attention. Well, it's finally done—let's go fly a kite.

To my partner and agent, Marc Davison: Your vision, efforts, and unique skills brought a local yokel writer of small-town press articles to the level of nationally syndicated columnist. What's more, you opened the doors to the inner sanctum of a major publishing house, ushering this book from mere concept to printed reality.

To my friend and fellow veteran home inspector, Dwayne DeVries: You've been an indispensable mirror and sounding board for ideas since my fledgling days of crawling under houses. We've worked together and camped together. Your proofreading of this text was vital, and your Morro Bay vacation home provided the quiet sanctuary necessary for the completion of this work.

To Dr. Robert Blodget, friend, Cal Poly professor, and personal computer mentor: Without your technical advisement and emergency rescue services, these creative efforts might have vanished amid the vast, unfathomable ethers of the unseen techno-void.

To Jim Turner, president of the California Real Estate Inspection Association and coauthor of my next book: Without your contribution of numerous field photos, this book might have been a dry landscape of black and white typography. In addition to these illustrative materials, I am grateful for your sincere encouragement and friendship.

To Mike Casey, president of the American Society of Home Inspectors: You are a fountainhead of encyclopedic knowledge to the many home inspectors and others who look to you for verifiable, authoritative information. I mailed advance copies of this book to a number of select individuals for proofing and review. A few suggestions trickled in, but you provided an avalanche of critical advice. What's more, you did it on short notice. The value of your contribution is significant and appreciated.

To Kevin O'Malley, founder and president of Inspection Training Associates, the leading home inspection school in the United States: Thanks for your encouragement, for the contribution of numerous field photos, for including this book among the educational materials recommended to your students, and for all you do toward the betterment of the home inspection profession.

To Gregg Cobarr of Cobarr Photography in Templeton, California: Your portrait of the House Detective in action has graced the homepage of <www.housedetective.com> for several years and now complements the front cover of this book. Thanks for giving star appeal to an average looking guy.

And above all, to the scores of straight-shooting real estate agents and brokers who continually recommend the most thorough home inspectors to their clients; who set aside the shallow warnings of misguided colleagues whose selfish plea is to avoid the so-called "deal killers"; who place the long-term interests of their clients above the immediate desire to clear a commission check; who make unabridged defect disclosure a vital imperative of their committed service to clients; who represent their clients with uncompromised integrity and truth, assuming the role of advocate rather than salesman. Truly, you are the unsung champions of the real estate profession and worthy of thanks. Sadly, you do not represent the totality of your profession, but you certainly reflect the best among our ranks. To those of you in my immediate sphere of business, your confidence and referrals have provided the experiential basis for writing this book. But beyond that, you exemplify in all that you do the moral standard that is wanting in so many areas of American commerce and culture: the behavioral model for all professionals who truly advance what is honorable and just. This book is about the values you represent, and for that—for your adherence to honesty and fairness in your daily pursuits—I offer my utmost respect and appreciation.

CONTENTS

Every house is a silent edifice of unspoken secrets. Drawing forth its voice; causing it to reveal its unknown blemishes; weighing the import of its major and minor confessions is the ultimate imperative of every homebuyer and is a primary theme of this book.

Property defects come in all sizes, shapes, severities, and costs. Some are obvious and apparent; others are elusive, except to the eye of a qualified professional. There are common visible problems involving deferred maintenance and routine wear and tear—the amateur handyman repairs. But there are also items of greater concern: major construction defects, structural inadequacies, safety violations, substandard materials and workmanship, unpermitted additions, and other conditions of significant financial consequence.

The vast array of potential defects is limitless, wide ranging, and often deceptive in appearance. There are problems that are readily apparent, and others that elude easy perception. Some, in fact, are undiscoverable without dismantling portions of the construction. There are faulty conditions that appear alarming to the uninitiated, such as wall and ceiling cracks; yet these might be identified by a qualified inspector as common cracks resulting from normal building stress. In contrast, there are seemingly minor symptoms, such as rubbing doors and windows, that might indicate major building settlement. And there are critical safety issues that would escape the attention of the average homebuyer, such as internal defects in fireplaces, substandard wiring in electric service panels, or faulty exhaust venting at gas furnaces— conditions that could be life threatening and might go unnoticed until found and reported by a qualified inspector.

All homes, regardless of age or condition, harbor a short, medium, or long list of such defects. Learning which of these potential problems underlie the attractive surface of the new or used home you plan to buy can determine the nature of your post-escrow experience—whether you will be happy and satisfied with your wise and well-informed purchase, or frustrated and overwhelmed when the true character of your acquisition becomes apparent.

A buyer's first line of defense against such loss is the process known as *home inspection.* When you hire an inspector, you employ an investigative expert to scrutinize the property before you finalize the deal. The information provided by a competent inspector enables you to make an informed purchase decision and avoid costly errors. With the understanding that post-escrow shock is needless and avoidable—there are professionals ready and able to assist you in the inspection process—this book will prepare you, the homebuyer, to:

- Protect yourself from undisclosed defects.
- Select the most qualified home inspector.
- Avoid lesser-qualified home inspectors.
- Avoid conflicts of interest between inspectors and agents.
- Increase your understanding of the inspection process.
- Know what to expect from a competent home inspector.
- Ensure that your inspector checks everything that warrants consideration.
- Gain more from your home inspection through direct participation.
- Be ready to catch the problems before they catch you.

WHAT THIS BOOK IS AND IS NOT

These pages are not intended as an instruction manual for those who wish to inspect a house. Excellent volumes have been written for that purpose. Although such books are useful and informative, it is the opinion of this author that homebuyers can be misled by materials that instruct them in the performance of their own home inspection. Furthermore, this book is not restricted merely to the subject of home inspection. Although home inspection is discussed at length, the purpose here is much broader and is multifaceted in scope. It is intended to:

- Expose the inner workings of the real estate disclosure process, within and beyond the confines of home inspection.
- Address all essential aspects of home inspection procedures as they relate to the needs and interests of buyers, sellers, and other parties to real estate transactions.

- Unveil the complex interrelationships and conflicts of interests that exist among buyers, sellers, home inspectors, agents, and others.

- Reveal the lesser known complexities and entanglements of defect negotiations, conflict resolutions, and other disclosure-related difficulties that, until now, have been fully observed only by home inspectors.

- Forewarn and forearm homebuyers against the common land mines and pitfalls that result in undisclosed property defects and train and equip buyers to sidestep these costly and avoidable traps.

Above all, the intent of this book is to reveal that every home whispers the truth of its own imperfections; and it is possible to hear that voice above the din of home-buying exuberance.

CHAPTER ONE

A SHORT HISTORY OF HOME INSPECTION

Disclosure marks the historical turning point in American real estate.

To homebuyers of the early 1900s, property inspection was unknown, unimagined, and seemingly unnecessary. To people of that simpler era, the main concerns were secure foundations and roofs that would not leak. Litigation was usually the last thought on anyone's mind. The worst drawback to a prospective home was having the outhouse more than 50 feet from the back door.

In the ensuing decades, home-buying changed dramatically from a simple, casual exchange to a complicated, legalistic process; from a personal handshake to an intricate complex of fine-print procedures signed in triplicate, witnessed by notaries, reviewed by attorneys, evaluated by appraisers, overseen by escrow officers, underwritten by title insurance companies, and dominated by disclosure requirements.

Most of this change occurred within very recent decades. For more than half a century, real estate complexities increased at a moderate pace, as did property values. By the mid-1960s, the purchase price of a home was barely more than two years' income for one working person, mortgage interest rates were around 5 percent, and buyers were relatively unconcerned about routine property defects. The American Dream was affordable, and people accepted flaws as part of the bargain.

Then came the 1970s and societal changes went ballistic, affecting all aspects of business and finance. Home prices escalated to previously unimagined levels. With the expanded financial commitment of enormous down payments and burdensome monthly installments, people were less willing to accept homes in "as is" condition. Properties were expected to be in good repair, and buyers were less forgiving of undisclosed defects.

In response to these changes, contractors began to offer a new kind of service: physical inspections for homebuyers. These early home inspections were basic overviews concerned primarily with major structural and mechanical defects. Yet most people remained unaware that even such basic services were available, and the quality of these inspections, with few exceptions, was rudimentary at best.

Gradually, home inspections became more common, and with this growth came an increasing demand for ever more detailed inspections. When buyers were not satisfied, inspectors soon learned that unreported defects spelled financial liability and unwanted relationships with attorneys. With the onset of claims and lawsuits, the exactitude of inspections rapidly intensified.

As the demand for disclosure increased on all fronts, home inspections emerged as a significant new profession. The first generation of inspectors, conceived in the 1970s, included concerned practitioners who foresaw the need for meaningful standards of practice to regulate their new and evolving profession. Across the country, inspectors formed national and state associations such as ASHI, the American Society of Home Inspectors, and NAHI, the National Association of Home Inspectors. Also emerging were state organizations such as CREIA, the California Real Estate Inspection Association; TAREI, the Texas Association of Real Estate Inspectors; and others.

In the absence of state licensing, self-regulation by these associations did much to elevate the level of professional inspectorship. Formal Standards of Practice were drafted, as committees of leading home inspectors brought years of experience to the forefront. Ongoing education became mandatory for all member inspectors, and codes of ethics were set forth to govern professional conduct. This, of course, did not guarantee that all inspectors performed at optimum levels; no method of regulation could accomplish that. But for the first time, there were specific guidelines defining the performance of a competent home inspector.

As these transformations were occurring in the marketplace, government agencies and legislatures were riding the wave of change. By the late 1980s, many states were enacting seller disclosure laws, signaling the end of the "buyer beware" era. Previously, sellers could "spit shine" a defective home, declare that everything was perfect, and walk away free of consequences. New disclosure requirements altered that picture, providing legal culpability for sellers who failed to reveal known problems and setting new disclosure standards for agents and brokers as well. The problem with these requirements was that sellers and agents were often unaware of inherent defects.

Meanwhile, Texas led the nation by mandating state licensing and apprenticeship for all home inspectors within its jurisdiction. Other states followed suit, some requiring licensure and others merely setting regulatory standards. (See the Web site <www.housedetective.com> for a list of states that currently license and regulate home inspectors.) But in most parts of the country, home inspection remains a maverick profession, ungoverned except by voluntary membership in inspector associations and a willingness to abide by the standards established by those groups.

In the short span of 30 years, the property transaction process has been totally transformed. Fear of litigation dominates the marketplace, and active disclosure has been recognized as the best preemptive defense. Information is now the central contingency, casting home inspectors as center stage consumer advocates.

For buyers entering this new purchasing environment, the ability to find and select the best home inspectors is essential. The guidelines contained in the following pages will assist in making this choice a wise and beneficial one.

ASK THE INSPECTOR

Seller Dismayed Over Detailed Home Inspection

Dear Barry,

I nearly sold my home last month, but the deal fell through because of a picky home inspector. I can understand making sure that everything is built to code. But this home inspector seems to make a big deal out of every little thing that may or may not be the buyer's business. I mean, what does it matter if the roof is worn as long as it doesn't leak? And so what if the water heater is 18 years old if it works just fine? I think you guys go out of your way to impress people with how much you know.

Victor

Dear Victor,

The character of the real estate marketplace has undergone radical changes in recent years. The old "buyer beware" principle is no longer acceptable. In today's litigious world, a seller's responsibility is to disclose, and home inspectors help to fulfill that obligation. The more that is disclosed, the less likely you are to incur legal conflicts after the sale. Defects that are withheld by you or missed by the inspector are potential courtroom scenarios.

As to the kinds of defects that should be disclosed, there are no limits unless you like to gamble. Litigation has been defined as "the sport of kings," referring, of course, to its exorbitant cost. Unless you fancy yourself a jester, my advice is to avoid a "royal" experience.

Limiting disclosure to building code issues can be a costly mistake. Code requirements are designed to ensure safe and stable construction. But codes do not address the deterioration and wear that develop as buildings become older, nor are they concerned with the quality of workmanship.

As to your roof: It may not leak at present, but what if it leaks after the sale? Who will pay to fix it? And regarding your 18-year-old water heater: How long can you expect "old faithful" to continue working? If it breaks down after the sale, who will buy a new one? If leakage causes damage to the building, who will be liable? If faulty combustion or a congested pressure relief valve should result in personal injury or worse, who will pick up the tab?

Buyers are entitled to full disclosure when purchasing a home. As a seller, you may soon become a homebuyer yourself. That's when you'll want to know which components are safe and operational and which are likely to fail in the near future. From that perspective, the thoroughness of the home inspector may be viewed in a different light.

———————————

CHAPTER TWO

UNDERSTANDING THE HOME INSPECTION PROCESS

Home inspection is often a grand mystery to buyers and sellers.

THE BASIC PREMISE OF HOME INSPECTION

A simple analogy illustrates the central purpose and process of home inspection: *When you buy a car, you take it to your mechanic; when you buy a home, the mechanic comes to you.*

An auto mechanic provides a detailed analysis of a vehicle whose purchase is under consideration. Components normally included (to name a few) are the engine, transmission, drive train, brakes, and suspension. Essentially, all of the basic mechanical functions and safety features are tested and evaluated.

In like manner, a home inspector reviews and evaluates all of the observable physical conditions of a residential property from the chimney top to the foundation; from the roof to the site drainage; from the attic to the subfloor crawlspace (carefully avoiding resident black widows).

ASK THE  INSPECTOR

Know the Scope When You Get the Scoop

Dear Barry,

I thought my home inspector would fully review the property I'm buying but was amazed to discover how much he overlooked. His report contained nothing about the intercom, the cable TV hookups, the fish pond in the backyard, or the septic system. What's the point of having a home inspection if so many items are not even inspected?

Arletta

Dear Arletta,

If you had received a full oral exam from your dentist, but the report had said nothing about the tendinitis in your elbow, you would not have been surprised or disappointed because it would have been understood at the outset that orthopedic evaluation was not included as part of the service. In the same way, home inspections can appear thorough and exhaustive when there is a clear understanding of which property conditions are included in the inspection process and which are outside the scope of the inspection. When the parameters are not established and clearly defined, dissatisfaction is likely to ensue.

If you check the home inspector's contract and carefully review the text of the report, you'll probably find that the items you mentioned were listed as outside the scope of the inspection. Cable TV hookups and other low-voltage electrical equipment are typically not included in home inspections, whereas the primary electrical system for a home is an essential consideration. Intercom systems are typically not included because they are technically complex, requiring the services of an electronic technician. Fish ponds are generally excluded because they are peripheral amenities, rather than essential components of the residence. And septic systems require evaluation by a licensed septic contractor because the tank must be pumped to enable adequate evaluation.

You should fully review the inspection and report with your home inspector to gain a full understanding of which conditions were inspected and which were not. For evaluation of components that were outside the scope of the inspection, other specialists should be consulted.

COMMON MISCONCEPTIONS

Public awareness of home inspection has not kept pace with the growth of the industry. Numerous buyers enter the marketplace with limited knowledge and false perceptions of this consumer protection process. Many are surprised to discover the wealth of information a qualified inspector can provide. Others are disappointed because their expectations exceed the scope of home inspection standards. Some confuse home inspection with a termite report or a real estate appraisal, while others presume that their home inspector will evaluate structural engineering, geological stability, environmental hazards, and other conditions not within the scope of a home inspection. Some believe that home inspections are primarily for older properties, that newer homes are free of significant defects. There are those who regard inspections as a superfluous waste of money that provide no particular benefit to anyone. And finally, there are some who have never even heard of a professional property inspection.

Misperceptions such as these cause buyers to waive their right to a home inspection, not realizing that this is their last, best chance to obtain critical information on this largest of all lifetime investments. Some discover too late the benefits of a professional inspection, after they own the home; when problems become painfully and expensively apparent.

Brokers and agents have been frustrated by the unwillingness of some buyers to grasp and appreciate the practical need for professional disclosure. In fact, some agents have elected to pay for inspections themselves, rather than risk the liability of undisclosed defects. Unfortunately, there are also less principled agents who view home inspection and defect disclosure as threats to the completion of a real estate transaction. To these shortsighted individuals, home inspectors are regarded as "deal killers." Thankfully, not all agents are of that persuasion.

ASK THE INSPECTOR

An Agent Speaks Up for Home Inspection

Dear Barry,

I've been a licensed Realtor for 11 years and regard defect disclosure as an essential service to my clients. Like many other agents, I encourage every buyer to have a home inspection. It gives them the information they need to make a sound purchase decision, and it protects me and everyone else from legal problems later. Unfortunately, some buyers choose not to have an inspection, and this makes me uncomfortable. How can I and other agents better educate our buyers about the importance of a home inspection?

Connie

Dear Connie,

You've certainly got the right idea: Disclosure is the cornerstone of prudent, ethical performance in real estate.

Home inspection, in recent years, has emerged as a standard procedure in most real estate sales. Unfortunately, many buyers do not realize the depth of information a detailed inspection can provide. By declining an inspection, they unwittingly deny themselves a significant financial advantage—the opportunity to discover conditions that could impact the value, safety, and eventual resale of the property they are buying.

The three main reasons why buyers forego the benefits of a home inspection are these:

1. *Shortage of funds: Some buyers want to limit their purchase expenses, so they buy a home on faith. Everything appears OK on the surface, so they gamble, never realizing there are defects an inspector would have found— defects the seller might have paid to fix.*
2. *Brand new homes: Many buyers succumb to the common misconception that a newly built home is free of defects. The fact is, every home has a list of problems awaiting discovery, and new homes are no exception, regardless of construction quality.*
3. *Inspection by a friend who is a contractor: This is one of the worst inspection mistakes a buyer can make. General contracting is about how to build a house, not how to inspect one. It takes years of full-time practice as a home inspector to learn the finer arts of discovery. In the same way that a uniformed patrolman is not a homicide detective, so a building contractor is not an expert in forensic evaluation of property defects.*

Your challenge as a Realtor is to convince these buyers that a professional home inspection will provide tangible and meaningful financial benefits; that the cost of an inspection will be more than offset by the information obtained. The depth and detail of an inspection should be made apparent. An effective approach is to show the buyers a sample inspection report. Sit down with your clients and page through a report, pointing out the broad scope and comprehensive detail of the electrical, plumbing, heating, roofing, and foundation sections. Explain that sellers often agree to repair conditions found by the inspector, and that these repair costs typically exceed the price of the inspection. What's more, let them see how frequently safety violations are reported, conditions whose potential consequences far exceed monetary considerations.

The cost of a thorough home inspection is nominal in the course of a real estate purchase. For the protection it buys, it is the most cost-effective insurance available.

SCOPE OF A HOME INSPECTION

The purpose of a home inspection is to discover all significant defects that are visually discernible, that can be discovered without dismantling components of the property; without opening walls or ceilings; without excavating the grounds. The inspection process involves evaluation of foundations, site drainage, floor framing, plumbing and heating equipment, electrical systems, doors, windows, interior and exterior finish surfaces, fireplaces, attic construction, roofing, and much more.

Home inspectors test electrical outlets, check the operational condition of electrical fixtures, and observe visible wiring within electric panels and elsewhere. Inspectors check the operability of plumbing fixtures and built-in appliances. They evaluate the quality, safety, and general condition of exposed building components. Common safety considerations include spark arrestors on chimneys, firewalls in garages, smoke alarms in and near bedrooms, stair and deck railings, tempered glass, gas piping, and much more.

The conditions reviewed by a qualified inspector number in the hundreds and are more thoroughly detailed in Chapters 6 and 10 of this book.

WHEN TO SCHEDULE THE INSPECTION

Home inspections typically occur during the first ten days or two weeks of the purchase transaction. The time limit for having the inspection is usually specified in the contract. Missing the home inspection deadline places buyers at a disadvantage—they could forfeit the right to an inspection or the ability to negotiate the inspection findings with the seller. Therefore, the inspection should be scheduled as soon as possible after signing the purchase contract. Buyers who wait too long to call the inspector of their choice sometimes have to opt for someone who is less experienced and therefore less thorough. The best inspectors are in high demand and are likely to be booked when you need them. Therefore, time is of the essence when scheduling a home inspection. It should be done at the earliest possible time.

INSPECTION CONTINGENCY

In most cases, the sale is contingent on the buyers' acceptance of the inspector's report. This means that you, as buyer, have a specified number of days in which to accept or decline the property in "as is" condition. If you decline acceptance, you have five basic choices:

1. Ask the sellers to make a few repairs.

2. Ask the sellers to make many repairs.

3. Ask the sellers to reduce the sales price.

4. Ask the sellers to credit you the cost of repairs.

5. Decline to purchase the property.

If you request repairs or a price adjustment based upon the home inspection report, the sellers also have choices. They can choose one of the following:

- Agree to all of your requests.

- Agree to some of your requests.

- Agree to none of your requests.

- Tell you to take it or leave it.

The sellers' only obligation is to address defects that are named in the purchase contract or are required by state and local laws. If the contract specifies an "as is" sale, the sellers may refuse to make repairs of any kind or to adjust the price in any way. Lawful exceptions may include strapping water heaters for earthquake safety, providing smoke alarms in specified locations, or upgrading plumbing fixtures for water conservation.

ASK THE INSPECTOR

Buyer Wants to Increase His Wish List

Dear Barry,

My home inspector checked the house I'm buying and described the air conditioner as old, with limited remaining life. This did not strike me as serious, so I didn't ask the sellers to replace it. But then my homeowners insurance company said the unit is a fire hazard and declined to issue a policy unless the unit is replaced. I tried to add this to my list of seller repairs, but my agent says it's too late to do this. What do you recommend?

Paul

Dear Paul,

As a buyer, you can make any number of repair requests of the sellers, but they may not be obligated to comply. Such requests are usually negotiable and depend in large part upon the terms of the real estate purchase contract. If the property is being sold as-is, this is doubly the case.

If, in fact, the air conditioner is hazardous, replacement would appear to be a reasonable request. If your contingency period for approving the home inspection has not expired, you may be able to add this repair request to your wish list, but the sellers may still retain the right to decline. If they flatly refuse to replace the defective unit, you can attempt a compromise arrangement, such as sharing repair costs, but the outcome will depend upon the disposition of the sellers. If they are totally unwilling to cooperate, you may have to choose between paying for a new air conditioner or rescinding the purchase of the property.

HOURS NEEDED FOR AN INSPECTION

The duration of an adequate home inspection is at least two and one-half to three hours for one inspector to evaluate an average size home (up to about 2,000 square feet). Larger homes, properties with additional living units, and those that are complex or poorly maintained are likely to require more time. Inspections of short duration should be regarded with suspicion. A quick inspection is an indication that thoroughness has been compromised and that some conditions may have been overlooked. Exceptions to this rule include condominiums and cookie-cutter tract homes. Some of these may take only two hours, but in no case should any inspection ever take less time than this unless the writing of the report occurs at a later time or unless a contingent of inspectors are working as a team.

ASK THE INSPECTOR

Buyer Skeptical about One-Hour Home Inspection

Dear Barry,

We just bought a 2,500-square-foot home, and our inspector spent about one hour reviewing the property. Since this was our first home inspection, we had no idea that it was a rush job. According to our neighbors, their home inspection took more than three hours. Should we be concerned?

Carol

Dear Carol,

The best home inspector alive cannot perform an adequate inspection in only one hour, especially on a large home such as yours. It is physically impossible for anyone. In fact, any home inspector who performs one-hour inspections is misrepresenting the services offered, while shortchanging the interests of customers. Such inspectors should be enrolled in boot camp–style reprogramming or be driven out of town on a rail.

Even for a small home, two and one-half hours is the minimum time needed for an adequate inspection. A one-hour job means undisclosed defects. At this moment, there are problems in your home that were not reported by your inspector. If you hire another inspector—one who is truly qualified—additional defects will be found. I guarantee it.

For the sake of financial prudence, peace of mind, and your family's safety, a second inspection is strongly recommended. Furthermore, "Mr. One Hour" should be asked to account for whatever additional findings are brought to light. At the very least, a refund of the inspection fee would be in order.

Buyer Participation

The benefits of a home inspection are greatly magnified when the buyers are present. Failure to attend the inspection is a missed opportunity that can have significant consequences. This subject is discussed in greater detail in the following chapter.

INSPECTIONS CAN ALSO BENEFIT SELLERS

Home inspections are commonly thought to serve the interests of buyers only, and in most transactions buyers are clearly the primary beneficiaries of the disclosure process. But the belief that buyers are the only ones who enjoy the fruits of this process is a grave error. The positive benefits of total disclosure serve the needs of all parties to a transaction, even those of the sellers.

In the legal minefields of today's business world, undisclosed defects can have costly and disruptive consequences in the lives of those who have just sold their homes. Sellers generally assume, in the aftermath of a sale, that the deal is securely closed and finished, that all related issues are necessarily laid to rest. This presumed comfort, however, can be rudely interrupted. Undisclosed defects often rear their grotesque faces after a transaction is completed. Though the sellers may have been forthright in their efforts to disclose all known defects, claims and legal confrontations can override the best of intentions, producing long, bitter, and expensive conflicts.

In anticipation of such problems, some sellers have opted to hire their own home inspectors, prior to marketing their homes. In this way, they increase their knowledge of the specific conditions of their home; are able to make repairs in preparation for the sale; can provide total disclosure to buyers; minimize the likelihood of conflicts after the sale; eliminate the need to renegotiate the terms of sale after the buyers hire a home inspector; and engender the trust of buyers by demonstrating a total willingness to disclose.

In spite of these distinct legal benefits and marketing advantages, very few sellers assume the proactive position of hiring their own home inspector. In most cases, the benefits of home inspection are left to the buyers, providing them, rather than the sellers, the strength and advantages afforded by increased knowledge of the property. Home inspection is a valuable opportunity bypassed by the majority of those who sell their homes.

ASK THE INSPECTOR

Advantages of Presale Home Inspections

Dear Barry,

As a homebuyer, I can appreciate the benefits of a home inspection. As a seller, there is something about the process that seems unfair. I spent weeks negotiating the sales price and terms with the buyer of my home. Finally, we reached an agreement and signed a contract. Then came the home inspection, and the buyers asked for further price concessions because of some defects. Now it seems we have no deal after all. Isn't there some way to prevent this kind of double-dealing?

Marty

Dear Marty,

Your frustration is the common experience of many sellers. In the wake of a home inspection, renegotiation typically occurs, but I would hesitate to call it "double-dealing." Most purchase agreements are contingent upon the buyer's acceptance of the inspection report, which means that the deal you worked so hard to finalize was only tentative.

Fortunately, there is a way to prevent second-round bargaining, but it requires you, the seller, to invest in a home inspection of your own before you find a buyer. The up-front expense may be unwelcome, but the benefits are significant.

Typically, buyers obtain the home inspection, using it to their own advantage, as an avenue to a second round of concessions by the sellers. To circumvent this process, some sellers hire their own inspector when the property is listed for sale, enabling them to provide buyers with full disclosure of the property's condition. By having a presale inspection, sellers accomplish four worthy objectives:

1. Purchase offers from buyers are made with full knowledge of the property's condition. Once an agreement is reached, the sale can proceed without second-stage negotiations.
2. A presale inspection exceeds the legal requirements for seller disclosure. Going the extra mile to provide full disclosure limits future liability.
3. A presale inspection demonstrates to buyers that the sellers have nothing to hide. It promotes an atmosphere of trust in which to negotiate the terms of a sale.

4. *Buyers often accept property defects "as is" when they are initially disclosed. When problems are revealed later in the purchase process, repairs are usually requested.*

The case for presale home inspections is a strong one, yet very few sellers take advantage of this opportunity.

ASK THE INSPECTOR

Seller Worried about Disclosure Liability

Dear Barry,

I am planning to sell my home and am concerned about legal problems if the buyer finds defects after the sale. If I disclose all the problems I know of, this may not be good enough because homes are always developing one kind of problem or another. If I put "as is" or "needs work" in the sales contract, will this protect me from repair demands, or is there more that I can do?

Michael

Dear Michael,

In today's litigious battlefront, someone, it seems, is blamed for every unfortunate occurrence in the course of business activity and daily living. Sadly, there is no guarantee against disclosure problems after selling a home, but you can definitely improve the odds in very major ways. The key is to provide the most thorough disclosure you possibly can and to exhibit an unusual willingness to advance the disclosure process.

Begin by hiring the most qualified home inspector in your area, someone with a reputation for scrupulous detail. Once you've got the inspection report, attach a copy to your disclosure statement. Furthermore, explain in your disclosure statement that every effort has been made to discover and report all problematic conditions but that you urge the buyers to hire their own home inspector, to ensure that no significant defects were missed by your inspector. In this way, you will have documented an unusual willingness to disclose all problems. In the unlikely event that surprise defects should surface after the sale, who could say that you deliberately concealed the problems? Even if matters proceeded to legal action, your position would look very good to any fair-minded judge or jury.

3

ATTENDING THE HOME INSPECTION

*If you miss the inspection, you
may also miss the boat.*

Too many homebuyers miss a great opportunity by not attending their inspection. Sometimes this is unavoidable, due to geographical constraints, but whenever possible, buyers are strongly urged to participate in the inspection process. Being on-site during the inspection, viewing specific conditions in person, consulting with the inspector, asking questions, and obtaining advice greatly magnify the overall benefit to you, the buyer.

A home inspection is a fact-finding mission in which the inspector is your hired expert. It is an investigative adventure wherein you and the inspector jointly engage in the discovery process. Both of you are there for the same reason—to learn as much as possible about the condition of the property.

Prior to the inspection, most buyers make a purchase offer based upon a 15-minute walk-through or run-through. At that point, they know very little about a very expensive commodity. The home inspection provides buyers their only opportunity to slowly and methodically view and consider the object of their investment. During the inspection, they have hours to voice questions and concerns as they evaluate their prospective purchase. Buyers have even been known to point out conditions the inspector might otherwise have missed.

Buyer attendance enables the inspector to fully explain the meaning and importance of each condition noted in the inspection report. When buyers are not present at the inspection, conditions noted in the report must be read and interpreted without explanation. Lacking a verbal review of the findings, a buyer may overreact to minor disclosures while, at the same time, failing to appreciate the importance of more serious ones. The on-site review provided by your inspector may be the most informative aspect of the entire home inspection process. When circumstances prevent buyers from attending the inspection, a telephone conference with the inspector is strongly urged.

ASK THE INSPECTOR

Buyer Confused about Inspection Report

Dear Barry,

We hired a home inspector to check the house we are buying, but now we're confused about his findings. What exactly does he mean when he states that the shingle roof needs "a tune-up"? Also, he reported that doors and gates are not within the code and regulations. Are we being unreasonable to ask the seller to have these fixed prior to closing of escrow?

Rosalinda

Dear Rosalinda,

When a roof needs a tune-up, it means there are defects needing attention but conditions are not serious enough to warrant roof replacement. Instead, a roofing contractor is needed to perform routine repairs. It would have been better had your home inspector stated precisely what defects were observed, such as: "Some cracked shingles were noted," or "Some shingles are missing," or "Aggregate is worn at some areas of the roof." My advice is to call your inspector to learn precisely what was meant.

As to the disclosures about doors and gates, it is very unusual for a home inspector to refer to codes and regulations in a written report. The purpose of a home inspection is to report significant defects, not violations of code. Again, my advice is to call your inspector to find out exactly what was meant.

In addition, I'm wondering if you attended the inspection and received an oral review of these findings by the inspector. Maximum benefit is obtained from an inspection when you attend in person. Neglecting to do so can be a big mistake. Far more can be learned when the inspector explains the report than when you try to interpret the disclosures on your own.

WELCOME TO YOUR INSPECTION

Your home inspection is *your* exclusive event. It is strictly for your benefit, and your inspector should roll out the welcome mat. True professionals recognize this essential aspect of client service and actively promote buyer participation. Unfortunately, some inspectors prefer to work alone and may discourage your attendance; these inspectors should be avoided.

Inspectors who sidestep their clients fall into three categories:

1. Some lack necessary interactive people skills. They prefer to mail the inspection report, avoiding verbal explanations of any kind.

2. Some work with an eye on the clock. Having the client on-site takes time and can mean one less job and one less inspection fee in the day's schedule.

3. A few inspectors are more interested in the needs of agents than of buyers. They provide whitewashed reports to ensure future referrals. (This, of course, is a highly provocative allegation and, fortunately, applies to a very small minority of home inspectors and agents.)

A home inspector is a personal consultant, not a hired technician. Inspectors who are not willing to consult should find another profession, and prospective clients should find another inspector.

ASK THE INSPECTOR

Our Inspector Excluded Us

Dear Barry,

Our home inspection experience was very disappointing. The inspector didn't let us know when the inspection was taking place. He just mailed us a report. When we complained, he said that's the way home inspections are done. This doesn't seem right to us. The people who are buying our house attended their home inspection. Their inspector completely reviewed his findings with them. Isn't it reasonable that buyers should attend their own home inspection?

Clair

Dear Clair,

Home inspection is a service business, and service means meeting the needs of those who are being served. Your experience—being held at arm's length by your inspector—is unusual, unacceptable, and constitutes an impediment to the essential goal of informing you about the home you are buying.

Home inspection is not a mere mechanical function. It is a multifaceted process that requires personal involvement. Inspectors are consultants. They are educators. Their purpose is to facilitate a comprehensive understanding of property conditions for homebuyers. The fulfillment of this objective is magnified when you attend the inspection and diminished when you are denied the opportunity to participate.

Your home inspector needs to rethink his relationship to customers, and you should insist upon a private, sit-down review of his report.

———————————

CHAPTER FOUR

CHOOSING THE RIGHT HOME INSPECTOR

Home inspectors are not created equal!

The above statement is a warning and should be taken seriously. A home that is inspected by two different inspectors may not produce equivalent reports. The roof defects revealed by one inspector may not be discovered by another. Plumbing, electrical, or heating problems disclosed in one report may not be mentioned in another, or they might be interpreted or emphasized differently. As a buyer preparing to make the largest financial commitment of your life, you cannot afford incomplete or incorrect disclosure. You are not looking for a partial list or even a nearly complete list of knowable faulty conditions. You need the full, unabridged story. Just one omitted item could adversely influence your purchase decision and lead to years of financial grief. Therefore, choosing the right home inspector is critical.

In every profession, some practitioners inevitably outshine others. This applies to all fields of activity, from medicine to farming, from mechanics to teaching, from politics to charity. Among home inspectors, professional disparity is broad and significant because there is no common background or educational experience that prepares inspectors prior to their commencing business. Some begin their careers as carpenters, others as heating contractors, architects, structural engineers, roofing contractors, plumbers, electricians, and so on. Each brings to the profession one or two areas of expertise, with a general or moderate knowledge of other related fields. But no inspector can be an expert in all of the structural, mechanical, and operational aspects of a home. Therefore, *basic building knowledge* is the first variable among inspectors.

The second and more essential variable is *the ability to inspect*—that is, to detect and recognize deficiencies when they are encountered. This does not come automatically with building knowledge. It is an acquired skill, developed by practice over a span of several years. Finding the inspector with the strongest balance of pertinent building knowledge and practical inspection experience can make the critical difference in obtaining full disclosure of a property's condition.

To enmsure that you choose a *qualified* home inspector, each prospect should be interviewed with the following criteria in mind: (1) professional affiliations; (2) inspection experience; (3) errors and omissions insurance; (4) building code certification; and (5) formal home inspection training. In addition, when selecting a qualified inspector, you should (6) ask for a sample report; (7) choose your own inspector; and (8) avoid price shopping.

Let's examine these in order.

PROFESSIONAL AFFILIATIONS

As stated in Chapter 1, inspectors in most states are neither licensed nor regulated. (See the Web site <www.housedetective.com> for a list of states that currently license and regulate home inspectors.) In most areas of the country, the only practical standards for home inspectors are those enacted by professional associations such as the American Society of Home Inspectors (ASHI) or the National Association of Home Inspectors (NAHI). To acquire membership in these associations, an inspector must pass a written test and must have performed at least 250 home inspections. Maintaining membership requires adherence to mandatory standards of practice, compliance with a professional code of ethics, and participation in ongoing educational programs, all of which significantly improve the quality of a home inspector's service. When you choose an inspector, specify those who are members in at least one of these recognized guilds. But beware of the following:

- *Membership pretense.* Some inspectors may claim adherence to association standards without maintaining actual membership. This is a way of appearing to be professional without the same level of accountability or relative knowledge possessed by members. The wording of an inspection company's advertisements is sometimes a dead giveaway. They may say "Inspections performed to ASHI standards," yet make no mention of ASHI membership. Such business practices are unethical and should be viewed with suspicion.

- *Membership not a guarantee.* Although the best inspectors are members of established associations, not every member is guaranteed to be a top-quality inspector. Therefore, the following qualifications should also be carefully considered.

ASK THE INSPECTOR

Buyer Wonders: What Is an ASHI?

Dear Barry,

Now that I'm buying a home, my agent says I need to hire an ASHI home inspector. When I asked her what the heck is ASHI, she didn't know quite how to explain it. Is ASHI some kind of state licensing, or what?

Del

Dear Del,

ASHI is not a governmental licensing agency. It is a private, national association of professional home inspectors whose primary purpose is to provide meaningful professional standards for a largely unregulated industry.

Home inspection is a relatively new profession, having emerged in the 1970s, grown and developed in the 1980s, and become a standard part of most home purchase transactions by the mid-1990s. Whereas most old and established professions are licensed and regulated by one bureaucratic monolith or another, home inspectors have enjoyed a free hand at developing, evolving, and self-regulating their practices in most states. In some ways, this unrestricted business activity has enabled the profession to find its proper function and placement in accordance with the needs of the home-buying public, developing and evolving in response to market forces and common business sense. On the other hand, the lack of regulation has also allowed individuals of lesser abilities and questionable motives to add elements of disrepute to this emerging field. In response to this disparity, the better-qualified members of the industry cooperated in drafting meaningful standards for the general practice of home inspection. Hence, the advent of the American Society of Home Inspectors (ASHI).

In the absence of governmental policing, ASHI emerged in the late 1970s as a major positive influence but was not alone in its pursuit of meaningful home inspection standards. Promoting the betterment of the inspection industry in like manner were NAHI, the National Association of Home Inspectors, and various state organizations such as CREIA, the California Real Estate Inspection Association, and TAREI, the Texas Association of Real Estate Inspectors. These organizations and others have been primary agents for elevating the profession and addressing ethical shortcomings and performance shortfalls within the industry. Their approach in this endeavor has been threefold:

1. To set standards of practice for the industry—defining the scope and limitations of a substantial home inspection
2. To establish a code of ethics for home inspectors—encouraging honest and ethical business practices among member inspectors
3. To stipulate ongoing education as a requirement for all member inspectors—mandating the furtherance of professional knowledge as a perpetual process

Although licensing has now been enacted in some states, most home inspectors continue to operate in an unregulated environment. (See the Web site <www.house detective.com>.) The only standards defining the performance of unlicensed inspectors are those that they accept voluntarily by electing to become members of such associations as ASHI, NAHI, CREIA, and TAREI. This does not mean that every member inspector is at the top of the trade, but those who are most qualified are found among the ranks of association members.

When choosing a home inspector, begin with a list of association members in your area. Then check to see who among these are the most experienced and have the most outstanding reputations for thoroughness as inspectors. And be sure to attend your inspection. That way, you'll learn as much as possible from your member inspector.

HOME INSPECTION EXPERIENCE

Home inspectors are often perceived as general contractors who happen to inspect homes, a view that betrays a critical misunderstanding of the home inspection process. *Home inspection consists primarily of investigation and discovery; contracting, on the other hand, involves the skills of construction and management.* Although building knowledge is essential to the practice of home inspection, construction itself has little or no relation to the practice of forensic analysis. A home inspector is primarily a property detective—someone who observes and ascertains defects. Inasmuch as a traffic patrolman is not a crime detective or your family physician is not a medical pathologist, likewise home inspectors should be viewed as diagnostic specialists distinct from other contracting professionals.

Although no apprenticeship standards have been established for home inspectors in most states, a realistic learning curve would include approximately 500 to 1,000 home inspections, with or without contracting experience. Furthermore, inspectors continue to refine their inquisitory skills the longer they are in business. Those who have not performed a large number of inspections are not yet qualified inspectors, regardless of their construction background. Some building contractors sharply disagree, which is to be expected. For those offended individuals, I propose the "House Detective Challenge": Call the nearest professional home inspector with at least three years of full-time field experience and a reputation for thoroughness as an inspector. Have the professional home inspector and you, the contractor, conduct separate inspections of the same building. When you are both done, compare the findings. The predictable disparity between the two reports will reveal the critical importance of home inspection experience.

ASK THE INSPECTOR

Contractor Gets a Crash Course in Home Inspection

Dear Barry,

One of my clients asked me to inspect a 36-unit apartment complex. Although I have no experience as a home inspector, I've been a licensed building contractor for many years. I'm familiar with all phases of construction and feel capable of performing an adequate inspection of these buildings. As this will be my very first inspection, I would appreciate some guidelines in setting a fair price for this service. How much money should an inspector charge for a job of this size?

Brian

Dear Brian,

Before you consider a price proposal for this inspection, let me emphatically advise you to reconsider an undertaking for which you have no specific training. The belief that construction experience is the only background needed to perform a home inspection is a common misconception and has led many contractors to encounter costly legal nightmares.

Home inspection is a relatively new profession, as compared with contracting, and its complexities are misunderstood by many. It incorporates an intricate combination of disciplines, skills, and learning, of which general construction is only one part. In addition to common construction knowledge, an inspector must recognize and evaluate various patterns of deterioration and wear affecting building structures and mechanics—conditions that would not be familiar to persons who deal primarily with new structures.

An inspector must also maintain an applied knowledge of building and safety standards relative to the age of each building, not just those that apply to new construction. If a property condition does not comply with current standards but was acceptable when the building was constructed, that should be reflected in the inspection report.

Above all, an inspector must have an acutely honed and thoroughly practiced sense of forensic observation, a skill that cannot be learned through construction experience. The capacity to identify subtle and elusive building defects is a unique craft in itself, developed through years of practice. A home inspector is primarily a professional investigator, not a construction technician.

When you undertake a home inspection, your clients will base major purchase decisions on your findings. Defects not disclosed in your report could be discovered at a later date, and you could be held accountable for the cost of correcting those conditions. Worse still, you could be liable for the consequences of undisclosed safety hazards. Consider these admonitions before you assume the complex demands of a highly specialized and unfamiliar profession. Your clients would be better served by someone thoroughly versed in the unique disciplines of home inspection.

———————————

ERRORS AND OMISSIONS INSURANCE

A vital consideration when choosing a home inspector is financial accountability. Undisclosed defects occasionally occur, even among the best inspectors, and these mistakes can involve substantial monetary costs. Because most inspectors are not endowed with "deep pockets," insurance is needed to underwrite liability in the event of a faulty or incomplete inspection. Inspectors who take their business liability seriously carry errors and omissions (E&O) insurance for these untimely mistakes, to ensure that funds will be available when undisclosed defects take on major proportions. Buyers should favor those inspectors who provide this protection.

It should be noted, however, that some very qualified home inspectors have chosen to conduct their businesses without E&O insurance. This decision is based upon the fear that insurance coverage attracts litigious attorneys and clients, just as sugar attracts flies. These inspectors prefer to discourage lawsuits by offering no pot of gold at the end of the rainbow.

Note: Two types of E&O insurance are available, one of which provides superior consumer protection. The best for consumers and inspectors is a "per occurrence" policy, because coverage remains in effect even after the inspector goes out of business. The other type of policy, called "claims made," can be effective on the date of inspection but invalid when someone is ready to file a claim, a deficiency not widely known among home inspectors.

ASK THE INSPECTOR

Understanding E&O Insurance

Dear Barry,

We purchased a home two years ago and hired a home inspector to find the hidden defects. Since then we've experienced numerous problems that were not disclosed in the inspection report. When we called the inspector, we discovered that he does not carry malpractice insurance. Aren't home inspectors required to be insured?

Robert

Dear Robert,

Insurance for home inspectors is commonly known as "errors and omissions" (E&O) insurance, not malpractice insurance. In most states, home inspectors are not required to maintain this type of coverage. You'll need to check with the appropriate government agencies for the standards where you live. In areas where insurance is not required, those inspectors who carry it do so as a matter of choice—for financial protection and as an expression of professional accountability. In so doing, they recognize that any inspector can make a mistake in the course of an inspection and that steps should be taken to safeguard themselves and their clients from damages that might thus be incurred.

Insurance coverage can be decisive when choosing a qualified home inspector. However, the lack of insurance may not reflect negatively on the qualifications of an inspector. Many inspectors decline coverage for fear that insurance invites the claws and fangs of hungry attorneys—the unfortunate effect of the litigious jungle in which inspectors and others must operate and survive.

BUILDING CODE CERTIFICATION

The primary focus of a home inspection is to discover significant building defects, not to evaluate building code compliance. This is a basic premise of the home inspection industry and is emphasized in nearly all home inspection contracts. Yet many property flaws are cited by home inspectors specifically because they violate the code. For example, if a guardrail is 34 inches high, a home inspector will cite it as having insufficient height. The building code will probably not be mentioned in the inspection report, but the disclosure is still based upon the code, which requires a 36-inch-high railing. Thus, an inspector's code knowledge can directly affect the discovery of faulty conditions. It also enables an inspector to advise safety upgrades in older homes, even though such improvements might not be legally required.

To ensure inspector competence in this area of building knowledge, seek someone with building code certification. This is the credential commonly held by municipal building inspectors who approve new construction. Although not a requirement for home inspectors, it identifies those who go beyond the minimum requirements of their profession to become competent, knowledgeable practitioners.

It should be emphasized, however, that many highly qualified home inspectors lack building code certification. Unfortunately, their code knowledge cannot be verified without earned documentation. My advice to these inspectors is to take the test and get certified. It may or not make them better inspectors, but certification, in the minds of many, speaks louder than words. Building a strong resumé is good for business, and preparing for the test will definitely increase code knowledge.

ASK THE INSPECTOR

Building Inspector Complains about Home Inspectors

Dear Barry,

I've been a city building inspector for 35 years and have a problem with some of you home inspectors. Many of you do a great job of finding building defects, but some of you make questionable calls when it comes to building code requirements. One problem I've noticed is that most of you are not even certified building inspectors, and this leads me to question your professionalism and qualifications. Why don't more of you guys learn the codes and get certified?

Jason

Dear Jason,

You raise a meaningful issue. Building code certification is an established requirement for municipal building inspectors throughout the United States and Canada. City and county building inspectors, such as yourself, are code compliance experts, empowered by government agencies to enforce code compliance as it pertains to all aspects of construction. Home inspection, on the other hand, is a private consulting service providing disclosure of property defects for persons who are buying homes and other types of property. The defined scope of a home inspection specifically excludes code compliance evaluations, which is why the majority of home inspectors are not code certified.

Problems arise, however, when the defects disclosed by home inspectors are cited specifically because they violate the building code. This is where home inspectors, not intending to perform code compliance inspections, find themselves unable to avoid such disclosures. It is an inescapable catch-22 of the home inspection process and is the best reason why home inspectors should enroll in building code classes and obtain code certification. It may not be required, but it would be a good step in the direction of improved professionalism.

FORMAL HOME INSPECTION TRAINING

In the early days of home inspection, most inspectors began their careers without any formal home inspection training. The exceptions were those who worked as employees of multi-inspector firms. But the majority merely entered business on the assumption that they already possessed the necessary skills and knowledge, based upon years of construction experience, and lacked nothing more than a checklist, a flashlight, and a ladder. Many of these risk takers finally managed, by hook or by crook, to become well-seasoned professional inspectors. Others, owing to their lack of training, were unable to attract repeat business or were sued out of business for defects they failed to report. By the early 1990s, this pattern began to change with the emergence of formal home inspection training schools. The pioneer among these was Inspection Training Associates, which today is recognized as the premier establishment for preparing individuals to commence meaningful home inspection careers.

The specific knowledge imparted by formal home inspection training provides entry-level inspectors with a foundational understanding of home inspection as a business, as a skill, and as a service. It sets them on the right track as they commence operation of their individual businesses, enabling them to learn the basics, without trial and error follies at the expense of their first several hundred clients.

When selecting a home inspector, ask if the inspector received formal home inspection schooling or served a training period with a multi-inspector firm.

ASK THE  INSPECTOR

How Can I Become a Home Inspector?

Dear Barry,

I've been a general contractor for over 20 years and would like to become a home inspector. Rather than just jumping in, I want to learn as much as possible about the business and about inspecting homes. What's the best way to get started?

Sandy

Dear Sandy,

You are taking the right approach: getting a good look before you make the big leap. The number one consideration when contemplating a home inspection career is liability. Your clients—mainly homebuyers—will base a major financial investment decision upon the information you provide. Incompleteness or incorrectness in your inspection report can have serious consequences for them and for you. Buyers who discover unreported defects after taking possession of a property can, at times, be very unforgiving. And that unforgiveness can arrive in the form of a demand letter from the buyers or, worse, from their attorney. Therefore, the more you do to prepare yourself, prior to entering the home inspection business, the more likely you will be to avoid such unpleasantries.

To begin, enroll in a home inspection training course. Inspection Training Associates is probably the best school available. You can visit them on the Web at <www.home-inspect.com>.

Next, contact your local chapter of the American Society of Home Inspectors (ASHI) and begin attending monthly chapter meetings. This will enable you to meet with experienced home inspectors, to participate in educational seminars, and to ask lots of questions. The more you learn about home inspection, prior to commencing business, the better service you will provide your customers and the more likely you will avoid legal trouble.

REQUEST A SAMPLE REPORT

The proof is in the product—in the style, format, and thoroughness of the report. So be sure to request a sample copy from each of the inspectors on your list of prospects. In reviewing a report, precise detail and extensive thoroughness are obviously important. However, an essential consideration is often overlooked: accessibility of pertinent information. How easy is it to find and understand the disclosed defects in the report?

Deciphering the inspector's meaning should not be a laborious effort. A quality report should be thorough and comprehensive, but also easily interpreted, making a clear distinction between defective building conditions and "boilerplate" verbiage. When immediate repairs are recommended or if experts are needed to effect such repairs, clear indications should be made in the report.

Some reports are so encumbered with maintenance recommendations, liability disclaimers, and general descriptions of the property and its components that pertinent information relating to faulty conditions is obscured. For example, some narrative reports camouflage critical disclosures in a jumble of "alphabet soup." A sentence disclosing a major foundation crack might be buried in a paragraph that describes the layout of the foundation system and the general style of construction. Disclosures of critical defects should be highlighted, not obscured. They should be underlined, printed in bold, separated from other verbiage, or in some way made to stand out visually from less vital information. They should not be adrift in a vast sea of words.

The same problem can be found with some checklist reports. For example, the checkbox that discloses a deteriorated plumbing system, one that needs replacement, may be no more distinct than the checkbox indicating the number of bathrooms or the location of the main water shutoff valve.

Reports of this kind, whether in narrative style or checkbox format, are confusing to buyers. Concentrated study is needed to ascertain the primary defects for which the home inspector was hired. The use of such reporting systems is a foolish practice; home inspectors who issue such reports are not thinking clearly.

Bottom line: A worthwhile report is not only detailed and comprehensive; it allows defect disclosures to stand out unmistakably, in contrast with less important data.

ASK THE INSPECTOR

Prudent Buyers Preselect Home Inspectors

Dear Barry,

We are in the process of house hunting and are wondering if we should select our home inspector before we find the home we want to buy. We'd just like to have someone lined up in advance, rather than scrambling for an inspector when we need one. Do home inspectors mind answering questions about their qualifications and providing references?

Jenny

Dear Jenny,

Your forward-thinking approach is unusual and commendable. Most homebuyers give no advance thought to the selection of a home inspector, but rely instead on last-minute, secondhand recommendations, usually from their agent. The results of this approach are sometimes satisfactory but many times disappointing. To better your chances of having a quality inspection, advance shopping is a prudent course.

To begin, ask your agent for a list of available inspectors in the area. Stress that you want to know who are the most qualified and experienced inspectors, the ones with reputations for thoroughness. Then make a few phone calls. Most home inspectors will gladly take the time to convince you of their qualifications. If an inspector is not comfortable with this or is unwilling to provide references or other evidence of qualifications, that's not the inspector for you. Just scratch that name off the list.

Primary considerations are years of experience, number of homes inspected, affiliations with recognized home inspection associations, errors and omissions insurance, willingness to have you present at the inspection, and readiness to discuss your needs and concerns on the phone.

And be sure to ask for a sample report. Seeing firsthand how the inspector presents the findings and discoveries will demonstrate the depth of the inspection and the manner in which the disclosed information will be conveyed. The report format should accomplish three objectives: (1) It should be thorough; (2) it should meet the standards of practice of ASHI, NAHI, or an equivalent association; and (3) it should be easy to understand.

Remember, this inspection is your best chance to learn about the home you plan to buy. A mistake at this stage can have costly consequences, so take your time and choose wisely.

CHOOSE YOUR OWN HOME INSPECTOR

When choosing a home inspector, don't rely on others to make your selection. The final choice should be your own. New and inexperienced inspectors often obtain recommendations from agents, regardless of competence or lack thereof. Although some agents recommend home inspectors on the basis of meaningful qualifications, others formulate their "preferred inspector" lists on the basis of discounted inspection fees or other questionable criteria.

When you hire a home inspector, you want the most meticulous, detailed inspector available—the one who will save you from costly surprises after the sale. As stated earlier, some agents regard the best home inspectors as "deal killers" or "deal breakers." But don't be misled by such labels. Deals are killed by major defects, not by thorough inspectors. Those with "deal-killer" reputations are usually your best prospects for comprehensive disclosure and superior consumer protection. In most cases, meticulous inspectors do not cause the death of a deal, but they definitely provide the most complete presentation of pertinent information about the property being purchased.

ASK THE INSPECTOR

How to Avoid a Home Inspection

Dear Barry,

As a real estate broker, I've had problems with home inspectors. It's understandable that major property defects should be disclosed, but why do some inspectors have to broadcast every little picky detail? And when problems are disclosed, why do they have to go into lengthy explanations? I say, fewer words would be less scary to my buyers. When reporting a problem, a home inspector can say, "Boo," or he can say, "Boo!Boo!" if you know what I mean. Earning a living is hard enough without having to deal with excessive disclosure. What can agents do to get you guys to back off?

Shelley

Dear Shelley,

In recent years, acceptance of home inspections and defect disclosure has become standard operating procedure for real estate professionals. But not all agents and brokers view home inspections with the same attitude and perspective. For some, there is the honest desire to provide full disclosure for their clients. For others, avoiding disclosure liability is the foremost consideration. For the misguided remainder, home inspections are little more than troublesome "deal killers"—thorny obstacles that threaten the process of closing the deal and securing that glorious commission check. For agents who long for the "used car" good old days, I offer this simple threefold technique for avoiding the troubling impediments posed by disclosure of all those picky physical defects:

Step 1: Never mention home inspection unless your buyer mentions it first. Fortunately, a few homebuyers still have no idea what a home inspection is. In those cases, consumer ignorance is on your side. Just do your due diligence walk-through inspection prior to closing the deal, and hope for the best.

Step 2: If the buyer suggests having a home inspection, explain why the house in question doesn't need an inspection. Here is a sample list of plausible reasons you can offer to forego an inspection:

- The house is too new to have any significant defects.

- The house is old and therefore should not be expected to be in perfect condition.

- *The seller has taken good care of the home, so defects are unlikely.*

- *The seller refuses to fix anything, so there's no reason to have an inspection.*

- *The house is priced below market, so there's no point expecting the seller to make further concessions.*

Note: Don't limit yourself to this summary excuse list. With some creative rumination, you can devise pretexts of your own.

Step 3: If the buyer insists on having an inspection, all is not lost. Many inexperienced home inspectors provide limited disclosure of defective conditions. In fact, selection of an unqualified inspector is actually quite simple: Just look for someone who is new to the business or who does inspections as a part-time occupation. When in doubt, ask the inspector how many homes he or she has inspected. Stick with the low numbers and you should be able to grease that buyer through an easy close.

Obviously, I'm being facetious. The fact is, most agents and brokers have learned the solid-gold value of a detailed, professional home inspection and routinely promote quality inspections as a standard way of doing business. My advice is to get in step with the winners. Try representing the best interests of your clients, and become a home inspection advocate. The lawsuit you prevent may be your own.

AVOID PRICE SHOPPING

Inspection fees vary widely. The price of a quality inspection is typically between $225 and $350 for an average-sized home. Lower fees should be viewed with caution, as they may identify those who are new to the business or who spend insufficient time inspecting the property. A home is the most expensive investment you are likely to purchase in a lifetime. One defect missed by your inspector could cost 100 times what you might save with a bargain inspection. In the final analysis, the best method of price shopping is to shop for quality.

ASK THE INSPECTOR

Quality Home Inspections Are Not Cheap

Dear Barry,

I recently moved to a rural area and was shocked to find the average price of a home inspection to be $250 to $300 or more. Before leaving the city, I was able to hire an inspector for only $99 and was fully satisfied with his work. How can small town inspectors justify charging more than twice the fee of a big-city home inspector?

Bruce

Dear Bruce,

Funny how y'all big-city folks think the only quality service available is uptown and nowheres else. There's an old adage goes like this: "As ya remit, so shall ya git." My granddaddy said that.

So happens, I know some "big-city" inspectors. Met 'em at a few seminars hosted by the American Society of Home Inspectors. Those are the powwows where we country bumpkins learn all the new-fangled inspection laws and techniques. Funny thing is, the big-city inspectors I met seem to charge the same as we do here in the sticks.

So as I'm sittin' here on the porch, wearin' my smelly overalls, and sucking on a weed, I gotta ask me this here question: What kind of inspector did a highfalutin sophisticate like yourself hire for 99 bucks?

Well, come to think of it, I used to live in the big city myself. Owned a construction business in L.A., and as I recall, there were two kinds of home inspectors available: full-time professionals and fledgling or part-time inspectors.

Fact is, most major cities suffer from a glut of home inspectors, some of whom are out-of-work contractors looking for a midlife career change. These entry-level inspectors generally invade the marketplace with little or no home inspection experience and no established clientele. To lure business away from the experienced and established competition, they typically offer underpriced inspections ($99 to $150) or other commercial inducements.

Price competition among inspectors should serve as a red flag to anyone seeking a thorough inspection. A detailed inspection takes a minimum of two and one-half to four hours. Add travel time and general business overhead (not to *mention liability insurance), and it appears unlikely you will find a qualified inspector for a mere $99.*

If you choose to save $200 on the inspection of a six-figure investment, you must be a gamblin' man. But just remember, the stakes in this game are high. The chances your inspector won't miss a few property defects are about as slim as dry corn silk on a hot July day. And months or years could go by before you discover the problems your inspector missed.

A common misconception is that anyone with a general contractor's license is qualified to inspect a home. This is as reasonable as assuming that anyone with a medical degree is fit to perform brain surgery. So before you consider price, look for qualifications. And remember: There are new home inspectors, and there are true home inspectors. But there are no new, true home inspectors.

It only takes one problem with the plumbing, electrical, heating, roofing, or foundation systems to offset the value of a bargain-basement inspection. When you hire a home inspector, you want to know everything about that home—not almost everything, but every last important detail. One omitted disclosure could cost you 50 times the amount you think you're saving. It's just not worth the risk. In any part of the country—big city, small town, or in between—that just makes good common sense.

————————————

The foregoing standards and caveats enable homebuyers to separate the best inspectors from average ones. To obtain the most complete and comprehensive property evaluation available, the eight guidelines in this chapter provide a reliable and effective method of screening home inspectors. Be sure to use them.

CHAPTER FIVE

INSPECTING BRAND-NEW HOMES

The Trojan Horse was new . . .
and should have been inspected.

False assumptions can be the source of much trouble and loss. For buyers of brand-new homes, the most common false assumption is that new means perfect. The consequence of this erroneous belief is that most new homes are purchased without an adequate final inspection, and construction defects remain undiscovered until a later and less opportune time. Either a functional defect or safety problem becomes apparent after the home is purchased, in which case the builder, hopefully, will honor the warranty. Or upon resale of the property, years later, problems are finally discovered by a home inspector, but by that time the builder's warranty has probably expired.

There are three misconceptions that lead buyers and their agents to justify the purchase of a new home without the benefits of a home inspection:

1. The home was inspected and approved by the municipal building inspector.

2. The builder is ethical, competent, and has an excellent reputation for quality.

3. The home is fully covered by a builder's warranty.

Again we encounter assumptions, so let's examine each of them in the following sections.

ASK THE INSPECTOR

All New Homes Need Home Inspections

Dear Barry,

As a Realtor, I'm concerned about protecting the interests of my buyers and am trying to convince my clients to hire an inspector for a brand-new home. They feel that this is a waste of money because the building was just approved and because the contractor guarantees the construction for one full year. Can you please explain why buyers of new homes should hire a home inspector?

Tisha

Dear Tisha,

Realtors who endorse inspections for new homes are major assets to the clients they serve. The belief that any new product is necessarily flawless runs contrary to common sense and experience, as amply demonstrated at the return counter of any department store. When applied to new homes, the idea that new equals perfect can lead to costly mistakes.

Anyone who has worked in building construction can recall shortcuts and human errors that routinely occur, even among very well-built homes. Workers have bad days, materials have defects, details are sometimes overlooked, components are occasionally omitted, and municipal building inspectors typically have insufficient time to check every nook and cranny.

Contractor warranties provide a false sense of security because they can only be invoked when defects are discovered and reported to the builder. If problems are concealed in attics, subfloor areas, within chimneys, or in electric service panels, how can their existence be revealed without a professional inspection? Even when problems are exposed to view, discovery may require esoteric knowledge of construction standards. The average homeowner is not qualified to recognize technical building violations.

Unfortunately, new homes are generally presumed to be exempt from human error. Consequently, most are purchased without the benefit of a final exam, with the result that defects remain hidden for years. When the property is eventually resold, a home inspector finally takes a look; but by then, the builder's warranty has expired and the seller is stuck with repair costs.

Considering the size of the investment, assumptions about the quality of workmanship can be financially damaging. The cost of an inspection is incidental to the price of a new home. A qualified home inspector will most assuredly find items that need repair. Better to discover them before than after the sale.

_____

MUNICIPAL INSPECTIONS

Building inspections, as performed by the building and planning departments of various cities and counties throughout the country, can be (but usually are not) as thorough and exacting as one would reasonably expect. Regulatory agencies are usually underfunded and understaffed. Whereas a home inspector might spend three or more hours to perform a detailed evaluation of a single residence, the municipal inspector may have 10 to 20 homes to check in a day. Allowing for driving time, paperwork, and returning phone calls, as little as ten minutes may be spent inspecting a given property. Inspections of this kind can amount to mere spot checks. Worse still, in large subdivisions, sample inspections are typically conducted at a representative number of dwellings, leaving many homes entirely uninspected. The result of this hurried and incomplete process is that defects and code violations of every kind may escape the scrutiny of those whose responsibility it is to police the safety and quality of residential construction.

In short, construction defects slip through the cracks and gaps of the building inspection process, leaving the home inspector as the consumer's last line of defense.

ASK THE INSPECTOR

Buyer Questions Municipal Building Inspections

Dear Barry,

We bought a brand-new home. After moving in, we found so many problems that we hired a home inspector. He found eight building violations and several instances of poor workmanship. We bought the house without a prepurchase home inspection because the construction had just been approved by the local building department. How could the municipal inspector have been so negligent?

Casey

Dear Casey,

In all fairness to municipal building inspectors, negligence is not the root cause of your problem. Construction defects do escape the official building inspection process, but the cause, in most cases, does not involve incompetence or a lack of professionalism.

Imagine, if you will, that you are a city or county inspector beginning a typical workday. Entering the office at 7 AM, you attend a staff meeting to discuss recent changes in the building code and some new administrative regulations mandated for your department by local politicians. Next, you reply to seven phone messages left on your voice mail the previous evening and work through a pile of paperwork on your desk. Finally, you're free to concentrate on your schedule for the day—a total of ten building inspections. Included are two foundation inspections for new homes, framing inspections for one apartment building and a room addition, a plumbing inspection for a remodeled bathroom, and final inspections for a small development of five new homes. Good luck.

You are now an hour and a half into a demanding workday and haven't even begun your first inspection. Allowing an hour or more for driving, another hour for writing correction notices, and remembering that your return to the office must be at least half an hour before quitting time, your time allotment for inspections is a tight squeeze at best.

At today's staff meeting, you had suggested hiring three more inspectors to relieve an unrealistic workload. But the city council recently proposed a budget cut for your department. Instead of more inspectors, there could be at least one layoff by the next fiscal year.

So you do your best in the face of daunting odds and a dogmatic bureaucracy. With thousands of code requirements to enforce and not enough time for an in-depth inspection, you focus on major concerns and try your best to include the details. Primary considerations are foundation and structural issues, but in your rush to stay on schedule, other code violations may escape discovery.

In the rare cases where unreported defects have major consequences, negative publicity may issue from the pens of sensationalist news reporters. But in all fairness, much can be said in support of your work. The beneficial effectiveness of municipal building inspectors can be seen, in particular, when natural disasters strike populated areas. Earthquakes, tornadoes, and hurricanes test the true nature of American construction standards and building code enforcement. In countries without mandated building inspections, disaster casualties can number in the thousands. In the United States and Canada, where code compliance is policed in an incomplete but well-intentioned manner, deaths resulting from structural failures are few and sometimes nonexistent in most disaster situations. Municipal inspectors accomplish this miracle within the confines and limitations of an imperfect system.

Private home inspectors offer a supplement to this work, not an alternative, providing final analysis and review. Limiting their schedules to two or three inspections a day, home inspectors spend hours rather than restricted moments on each inspection. Without administrative and budgetary constraints, they can devote the time needed to conduct detailed, comprehensive inspections of new and existing construction. Both forms of inspections, municipal and private, complement one another as preliminary and final aspects of a total inspection process. Both provide immeasurable benefits to the home-buying public.

RELIABLE BUILDERS

The most ethical, qualified, and highly reputed builder may construct an excellent house, but no one can build a perfect house. To put it bluntly, the best builder remains human, as do all of the subcontractors, installers, technicians, and tradespeople who lend their services to the construction process. The newly finished home can be of the highest quality, but as with all things made by hands, errors are inevitable. The construction of a home involves innumerable details, and the various persons performing and overseeing the work have neither the time to scrutinize every aspect nor the infallibility to get it all right the first time. The nature of life and of humanity dictates that mistakes will occur in the construction of anything as large and complex as a home, regardless of the abilities and ethical concerns of those involved.

Again, construction defects slip through the inevitable crevices of the building process, leaving the home inspector as the consumer's last line of defense.

ASK THE INSPECTOR

Excellent Builders Welcome Home Inspectors

Dear Barry,

Some of your past articles have recommended home inspections for brand-new homes. We're presently purchasing a new home that is being built by a contractor with the highest reputation for quality workmanship. Everyone raves about his work. We feel that an inspection in this case is not necessary and would needlessly insult the builder. Don't you think this might be an exception to your rule?

Janice

Dear Janice,

In the home construction business, there are more than a few top-drawer builders, men and women with the utmost integrity and professional qualifications who produce homes and other buildings of the most exemplary quality. Apparently, you are the fortunate beneficiary of one of these excellent people. But no matter how qualified and exacting your builder may be, no matter how much concern he may focus on absolute perfection and exactitude, in all likelihood he is still human. With the understanding that no divine deities are presently engaged in the home construction business, it can be safely assumed that there are no perfect builders, even among the gifted best.

Here is a typical example: A first-class general contractor built a home as his personal family residence. Because it was his own, it was not only well built but was given that extra measure of attention to exacting detail. It can truly be said that he constructed a first-class, exceedingly excellent home. However, when he sold it three years later, the buyers hired a home inspector, and the report contained several items that totally surprised the contractor-seller. Among these were three significant safety issues. First, the large picture window next to the master bathtub was not made of safety glass. The builder probably ordered and paid for tempered glass, but that is not what was installed, and somehow no one noticed this discrepancy at the time of construction. Second, the metal chimney for the fireplace was in direct contact with wood framing in the attic. One inch of clearance was required for fire safety, but somehow this escaped everyone's attention when the house was built. Finally, the flue pipe for the water heater had not been securely connected. One of the fittings had separated, and combustion exhaust was venting into the building. Some workman had simply forgotten to install a few screws, and the builder, unable to be everywhere at once, failed to notice this one particular detail.

When home inspections are recommended for new homes, it is not because contractors and builders are not worthy of trust (although some individuals warranting scrutiny and suspicion are reportedly at large). Rather, it is because all builders are human—subject to occasional and unintended errors. It is because a home is too large and complex an object to be constructed without some defects having gone unnoticed, regardless of the integrity and ability of the builder. And keep in mind that your excellent builder is the director of the total project, not the sole practitioner of each detail of the work itself. Notwithstanding his very best efforts, he has to trust in the flawless performance of every subcontractor and the unerring workmanship contributed by every employee of those subcontractors.

As to the possibility that a home inspection will insult your builder: Professional contractors are often (but not always) very appreciative of the services of qualified home inspectors. A final home inspection can provide an extra measure of quality assurance, informing your builder and the various subcontractors of last-minute details needing adjustment or correction upon completion of the construction process.

BUILDERS' WARRANTIES

Warranties are wonderful when backed by ethical builders—those with reputations for quality work and a genuine concern for the satisfaction and financial well-being of their customers. Unfortunately, not all builders fit this admirable description. In too many cases, the compromised integrity of a builder can render a warranty worthless, leaving the buyers of a new home with costly defects, attorney bills, years of aggravation, and, in some cases, a property that cannot be resold. The sad stories that fit this pattern are endless. The best time to invoke the provisions of a builder's warranty is before purchasing the property, when the builder's desire to obtain your purchase money is a motivating factor.

When builders and other parties to the transaction are not concerned with your best interests, a home inspection prior to purchase is your best line of defense.

ASK THE INSPECTOR

The Problem with Homebuilders' Warranties

Dear Barry,

My agent insists that I hire a home inspector for the brand-new house I'm buying. This seems unnecessary because the builder fully warranties the home for a complete year. If anything goes wrong during that time, I can simply call the builder, and he'll fix the problem. With a warranty to cover problems, why should I spend money on a home inspection?

Jules

Dear Jules,

Builders' warranties are wonderful things, assuming that your builder is responsive to reported defects and assuming that you recognize the defects before the warranty period expires. Both assumptions warrant serious consideration.

Many builders provide honest and responsible warranty repairs when construction flaws are found. If problems are discovered after the sale, these contractors respond quickly and decisively—evaluating and repairing the defects discovered by the new owners. Unfortunately, there are also a number of builders whose warranty performances are less than admirable—those with a short-term view of the bottom line, with too many irons in the fire, or with a lack of empathy for the needs and concerns of others. They comprise that contingent of undesirables to be found in all professions—the ones who could use a rap on the knuckles with a stiff ruler or a swat with an oak paddle by an old-fashioned PE coach. In the absence of such discipline, a home inspection prior to purchase affords a buyer vital foreknowledge of imperfections and a distinct edge when negotiating for repairs. If repair requests are proposed to a builder as conditions of the sale, the buyers have leverage, and positive responses usually follow. On the other hand, when repairs are demanded after the sale, the response is consistent with the relative integrity of the builder—good, bad, or indifferent.

Another reason for inspecting a new home is unrelated to the issue of builder ethics. It involves the likelihood of defect discovery.

Not all construction errors are apparent or recognizable to the average homeowner. When defects are not functional in nature or are situated in concealed areas, they can elude discovery until long after the warranty period has expired. Home inspectors routinely evaluate such conditions: within electric service panels, attics, subfloor crawlspaces, air plenums, combustion chambers, and so on. They test the wiring of outlets and consider numerous aspects of plumbing, mechanical, and fire safety compliance. They check workmanship standards related to roof installations, wood framing, and countless other aspects of the building. Defects in such locations are seldom evident to homeowners and, therefore, would not be brought to the attention of the builder during the warranty period. Instead, they might be discovered years later, when the home was being resold, when the buyer's inspector finally brought them to light. Then, in the aftermath of warranty coverage, the sellers might be saddled with the repair costs.

These are the best reasons to provide yourself the financial and safety benefits of a professional home inspection, regardless of the coverage provided by a builder's warranty.

UNCOOPERATIVE BUILDERS

Most builders accept the home inspection process as a new aspect of an ever changing construction industry. Some even welcome home inspections as an added quality control service, providing final confirmation of completeness and correctness at the conclusion of a construction project. Unfortunately, a few rotten specimens can be found in this barrel of good apples—the shady dealers who give a good industry a bad name, employing varying methods and degrees of home inspection resistance and avoidance. These unfortunate practices range from benign but unmistakable unfriendliness to outright, teeth-clenched refusal to admit an inspector onto the construction site.

Some builders forestall home inspections until after the sale has been completed, convincing buyers to complete an as-is purchase. They leave buyers to hope that the findings of a later home inspection will be addressed in accordance with the builder's warranty.

Other builders have discovered a more a devious method of barring home inspectors from the site of a newly built home: Instead of openly declaring that the inspector is forbidden from the project, they mandate that each inspector possess a multiplicity of credentials and insurance policies far in excess of those any inspector or other business professional would be likely to have. In this way, they effectively screen out all potential applicants, regardless of the inspector's actual experience or qualifications.

Consumers have a right to question and evaluate whatever commodities they elect to purchase. If you buy a vehicle, you have it checked by your mechanic; that is normal, reasonable, and expected. When buying a boat, you call a surveyor; for livestock, there are vets. Likewise, buyers of new homes should be free to enlist experts of their own choosing. Builders who deny this basic right are not conducting business in a forthright manner and should be cautiously avoided.

Homebuyers who dismiss this warning do so at their own risk. Buyer beware.

ASK THE INSPECTOR

Builder Denies Access to Home Inspector

Dear Barry,

I'm purchasing a new home and want my home inspector to check it out before I close the deal. But the builder refuses to let him on the property and has threatened to charge him with trespassing if he's seen on the site. Other buyers in the subdivision hired this same inspector and the builder is irate because of problems that were found. The county inspector agreed with the home inspector's findings and made the builder repair everything. What is your experience in dealing with home builders? Do they have a right to tell us who we can hire for home inspections?

Steve

Dear Steve,

Refusal to allow a professional home inspector on a building project is legally questionable and ethically inexcusable. Unfortunately, the barring of home inspections has become a common practice in some areas of the country. Some builders disguise this dubious practice by setting unreachable home inspector standards. For example, a builder might say that home inspectors are allowed if they have engineering degrees, contractor licenses in all aspects of the construction to be inspected, and carry workers' compensation and liability insurance specifically for the site to be inspected. Obviously, no one can meet all of these standards, so the builder manages to preclude home inspection under false pretenses.

Honest and reputable builders are open and amenable to the home inspection process and typically afford inspectors free access and full cooperation. These builders regard a home inspector's report as a final pickup list, facilitating better relations with buyers and reducing the number of problems likely to surface in the aftermath of the sale.

In all fairness, it should be stated that some home inspectors have made overreaching repair recommendations on new homes, fostering bad feelings among builders, but this does not justify a carte blanche prohibition of home inspectors in general.

Your builder is apparently not dealing in a forthright manner. All new homes have defects that can be identified by a qualified inspector, and up-front contractors welcome such input. You can use legal means to enforce your right to use a home inspector of your choice. However, you might also consider whether you want to buy a home from a builder who is unwilling to address defects. To what extent will such a builder respond to problems that develop after the sale? This situation might be a welcome warning, a hint to begin house shopping in another subdivision.

NEW HOMES NEED TO BE INSPECTED

The foregoing perspectives underscore the importance of hiring a qualified home inspector prior to purchasing a new home. A thorough home inspection will disclose those defects not discovered by the municipal building inspector. It will produce a final pickup list for the high-quality homebuilder and will prevent low-quality builders from completing sales without addressing critical construction defects.

A competent home inspector benefits the buyer of a new home and, in every case, reveals conditions that warrant attention.

ASK THE INSPECTOR

Most Common Defect in New Homes

Dear Barry,

Your column occasionally mentions that all brand-new homes have defects and should be inspected before purchase. Out of curiosity, what are the top five flaws that home inspectors encounter in newly constructed homes?

Adam

Dear Adam,

As repeatedly stated, the critical importance of having a newly built home professionally inspected cannot be exaggerated. Buyers of new homes often discover defects after the purchase and wish they had hired an inspector. They bypass the opportunity to have an inspection because new homes just look so perfect, and because there is a general reliance on the municipal inspection process and the mandated builder's warranty. But regardless of newness or the integrity of the builder, all new homes have conditions that have escaped the various oversight processes of foremen, superintendents, and inspectors and that warrant upgrades, completion, or repairs.

In answer to your question, five common categories of typical problems in brand-new homes would include:

1. *Inaccurate or incomplete finish work*
2. *Various roofing defects*
3. *Faulty surface drainage around the building*
4. *Gas or electrical safety violations*
5. *Fire safety violations*

Other inspectors will no doubt wish to add to this list, and that's OK. In fact, the kinds of defects likely to be found in new homes cover all aspects of construction. Any component is a candidate for possible defects, and you never know where the problems lurk until you have a professional inspection. Buyers of new homes should take heed: There is no such thing as a flawless house, and it's better to find the flaws before closing the sale than to chase a busy builder after you assume ownership of the property.

———————————

CHAPTER SIX

SCOPE AND LIMITATIONS OF A HOME INSPECTION

*Home inspectors are constrained
by human limits.*

The scope of a home inspection is not without boundaries. Unfortunately, many buyers don't realize the extent of these limits. As repeatedly stated in this book, a home inspection is a visual inspection only, limited to those aspects of a property that are accessible at the time of the inspection, to conditions specified in the standards of practice of the inspection industry, and to items mandated by law in some states. To ensure that buyers and other parties understand these bounds, home inspection contracts and reports specify particular aspects of a property that are included and those that are not included in an inspection. When these parameters are not clearly understood, needless conflicts can arise in the aftermath of a sale. For this reason, knowing the limits of your home inspector's responsibilities can be critical if you experience post-purchase encounters of the worst kind.

Professionals are generally employed with an implied understanding of their scope of work. When you hire a plumber, you know that your pipes and plumbing fixtures will be serviced, not your roof. When you engage your auto mechanic, it is understood that the functional components of your vehicle will be repaired, not the upholstery. When you visit your dentist, you are definitely not there for an eye examination. To hold these people accountable for problems involving roof shingles, seat fabrics, or blurred vision would be unreasonable. When hiring a home inspector, the same principle applies. There are conditions that fall within the defined scope of a home inspection, and there are others that do not.

49

An accurate understanding of the home inspection process is essential when buying real estate. Knowing what an inspector does and does not do broadens your knowledge of property conditions before you take possession; it alerts you to concerns that might need the attention of professionals other than your home inspector; and it prevents needless disputes after the sale is completed.

Notwithstanding the best efforts to define the scope of an inspection, some buyers are still surprised to discover that their inspector did not evaluate the underground sewer lines, the electric wires within walls, internal components within the furnace, or the geological stability of the neighborhood. Standard exclusions are reasonable, they are generally uniform and consistent throughout the industry, and in most cases they are clearly stated. To advance a better understanding of home inspection parameters, the following explanations are provided.

Someone asked why the home inspector did not inspect the rear portion of the roof. Roof is overgrown with vines.

ASK THE INSPECTOR

Understanding the Inspection Contract

Dear Barry,

During a recent home inspection, I had to review and sign the inspector's contract.

It was filled with so many limitations and so much legalese that I questioned the quality and thoroughness of the inspection itself. I checked with two other inspectors and found their contracts to be slightly different but just as detailed and complicated. Could you please discuss the various clauses in these contracts and why such heavy-handed documents are necessary?

Val

Dear Val,

A primary business concern among home inspectors is exposure to liability and the likelihood of eventual litigation. Least among these worries is the possible consequence of professional negligence, such as failure to disclose a significant property defect. The more ominous fear is the specter of a frivolous lawsuit arising from the unreasonable expectations of a misdirected buyer or the baseless demands of an overzealous attorney.

Today's business environment is commonly recognized as a wild litigious jungle, where predatory ambushes in the dense legal underbrush are to be anticipated. For home inspectors, exposure to attack and financial demise is a dreaded fear to be avoided, defined, and limited as much as possible. Hence, the lengthy and laborious legal clauses of the typical home inspection contract.

Although home inspection agreements vary widely in their specific contents, there are some common denominators. Among these are four categories of liability limitation:

1. Defining the scope and limitations of the inspection

    Most homebuyers have a vague concept of the general scope of a home inspection. The exclusions listed in the inspection contract can dispel uncertainties in this regard. For example, in most states, home inspectors do not inspect for termites and other wood-destroying organisms, as this practice is usually reserved by law for licensed pest control operators. Other common limitations involve engineering standards, geological stability, environmental hazards, zoning designations, lot line placement, low voltage electrical equipment, product recalls, and many more. Chief among home inspection disclaimers are conditions that cannot be seen because they are concealed within the construction, buried beneath the ground, hidden behind personal property, or otherwise unobservable. These and many other conditions are listed in contracts as being outside the scope of the inspection.

2. Setting a monetary limit on liability

    Many inspection agreements state a specific dollar maximum on liability, commonly a refund of the inspection fee or a multiple number times the inspection fee. In some states, this limitation has been upheld by the courts; in others, it has been rejected. Some inspectors have no such limits in their contracts because the deductibles on their errors and omissions insurance policies provide a reasonable ceiling for liability.

3. Establishing a means of dispute resolution (usually arbitration or mediation)

    Courtroom litigation and the discovery processes that lead to trial are among the most lengthy, costly, and frustrating means of conflict resolution. Even the winners are losers when the financial and emotional costs are *tallied. To avoid such ordeals, inspectors often prefer the less protracted processes of mediation or arbitration, as set forth in their contracts.*

4. Shortening the statute of limitations

Many states provide no statutory time limits on home inspector liability. Others have statutes of limitations that can expose an inspector to potential litigation many years after the inspection. Some inspection contracts address this by limiting liability to a specific time frame, such as one year. Enforceability of such clauses can vary from one state to another, and in some areas, from one court to another.

The cautious structuring of home inspection agreements, in most cases, should not arouse concern regarding the quality of the inspection being performed. These contracts are simply a reflection of the conflict-oriented business environment in which we live, a marketplace where every adverse event is "someone's fault"; where someone, somehow, must be held accountable. Home inspectors, along with the rest of us, are caught in this regrettable tangle.

To ensure that you receive a thorough and competent inspection, check the inspector's qualifications and reputation beforehand and read the contract carefully before you sign it. You can also request an advance copy of the contract for review by your attorney.

CONDITIONS WITHIN THE SCOPE OF A HOME INSPECTION

Those items typically included in a visual home inspection are as follows:

Exposed foundations. Portions of foundation systems that are aboveground and fully visible are included in a home inspection, whereas portions of foundations located belowground are not subject to inspection. With concrete slab foundations, very little is actually exposed. In such buildings, the inspector can look for cracks at interior and exterior walls, for floor cracks that are large enough to be visible through floor coverings, and for any other visible evidence of possible building settlement.

ASK THE INSPECTOR

Uncovering Hidden Property Defects

Dear Barry,

We bought our house five years ago. At that time, our home inspector seemed to do a good job, but now we've found a problem that was not listed in his report. We were recently redoing our landscaping, and the excavation revealed that part of the house is built on a slab floor but without a foundation. This is a severe construction defect and was never reported by our inspector. When we confronted him, he refused to pay for a new foundation. Shouldn't home inspectors be responsible for negligent work?

Marjorie

Dear Marjorie,

Your home inspector's failure to discover this foundation problem may not constitute negligent performance. Most inspectors conduct their work according to the standards of practice of the American Society of Home Inspectors (ASHI) or similar professional associations. In keeping with these criteria, a home inspection is limited to conditions that are visually discernable. Specifically excluded are conditions concealed from view, such as items contained within walls, ceilings, and floors, or, in your case, buried beneath the ground.

According to accepted industry guidelines, inspectors are not required to dismantle construction or excavate soil to discover problems that are not normally visible. The fact that your foundation problem remained undiscovered for five years and was only revealed by means of excavation indicates that the defect was not visually detectable.

To clarify the standards by which your home was inspected, take the time to reread the inspection report. Most reports specifically define the scope and limitations of the inspection. These parameters are generally outlined in the contract, as well as within the report itself, and nearly all contracts state that concealed items are outside the scope of the inspection. In addition, most inspection reports specifically identify ASHI standards, or those of an equivalent organization, as the basis upon which the inspection was performed. If these guidelines were laid down in a clear and understandable manner, then discovery of buried conditions would not be the responsibility of your home inspector.

Subfloor framing. Floor construction and other wood components in the subarea beneath a building are examined for damage, substandard construction or modification, moisture-related problems, and evidence of possible building settlement.

Site drainage. Ground surfaces and pavement are checked for signs of drainage toward buildings and for evidence of ponding or soil erosion. Areas below buildings are checked for evidence of water intrusion, ponding, or ground erosion. Water stains and musty odors inside buildings may also provide evidence of faulty site drainage.

Large notch in subfloor framing negates structural integrity.

Lawn area drains toward building.

Exterior walls and trim. Exterior building surfaces are inspected for damage, wear, faulty construction, substandard materials, the effects of weather and moisture, and evidence of possible building settlement.

Roofing systems. Roof coverings are inspected for damage, wear, faulty installation, and evidence of substandard materials. Gutter systems and metal fittings (known as flashing) are also inspected for faulty conditions and improper installation.

Substandard roof repair.

Attic space. The attic area is inspected for damaged or substandard framing and to determine the adequacy of insulation and ventilation. In addition, plumbing, electrical, mechanical, and chimney conditions within the attic are inspected.

Fireplaces and chimneys. Woodburning fixtures are inspected to determine general condition, proper construction and installation, adequate clearances to combustible materials, and compliance with common fire safety standards.

Damaged roof framing in attic.

ASK THE INSPECTOR

Why Didn't My Inspector Walk on the Roof?

Dear Barry,

Our home inspector did not go on the roof to inspect it. He just checked it from the ground and from his ladder. Is this OK, or do we have reason to question the thoroughness of the inspection?

Laurie

Dear Laurie,

Home inspectors typically inspect a roof by walking on the surface, as this is the best way to observe and evaluate all pertinent conditions. There are, however, six common conditions that would keep an inspector off the roof:

1. The surface is too steep to provide safe footing.
2. The surface is too high for access with a normal-length ladder.
3. The roofing is so deteriorated that foot traffic would cause further damage.
4. Surface conditions such as snow, ice, moisture, or moss make the roof too slippery.
5. The roofing consists of tiles or other materials that might be damaged by foot pressure.
6. The sellers have ordered the inspector to stay off the roof.

Barring these circumstances, any home inspector who won't take a walk on the roof should take a walk.

ASK THE INSPECTOR

Minor Repairs versus Structural Repairs

Dear Barry,

Why do home inspectors include minor defects in their reports? My house is being sold, and the buyer hired someone to do a structural home inspection. The inspector included ceiling stains and doors that rub. These are not "structural" problems, but they've started a chain of requests from the buyer to correct nitpicky details. Our contract does not spell out the difference between maintenance repairs and structural repairs. What can I do?

Linda

Dear Linda,

Your point is well taken, but with some important qualifications. Minor defects, such as rubbing doors, should not become the focus of a home inspection report. Such repairs are certainly not incumbent upon a seller. Ceiling stains, however, are indicative of past or current leakage, either at the roof or the plumbing system. Further evaluation of these is always prudent, and for this reason stains are typically disclosed by home inspectors.

Another item that needs clarification is your repeated reference to a home inspection as a "structural inspection." In a strict sense, the word "structural" is very limited in its scope, referring primarily to issues involving foundations, framing, and ground stability. A home inspection, however, encompasses far more issues than these, including, but not limited to, the plumbing, heating, and electrical systems, fireplaces and chimneys, roofing, built-in appliances, ground drainage, general safety compliance, and much more. In essence, the purpose of an inspection is to identify significant property defects that are visually discernible. Minor defects are typically included as a courtesy only. To limit the scope of a home inspection to purely structural considerations would drastically reduce the accepted standards of practice for a physical inspection.

Interior surfaces. Ceilings, walls, and floors are inspected for damage, wear, faulty construction, moisture problems, and evidence of possible building settlement.

Stairs. Interior and exterior stairways are inspected for damage, faulty construction, moisture-related problems, and compliance with common safety standards.

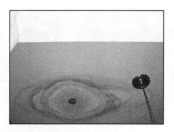

Water damage on ceiling indicates roof leak or plumbing problem.

Major stress cracks in brick chimney.

Stairway needs a handrail for safety.

Electrical system. Electrical evaluations include inspection of the wiring within breaker panels and fuse panels, inspection of the service lines to the property (unless buried), inspection of accessible exposed wiring, random testing of light fixtures and wall outlets, and observable compliance with common safety standards.

Plumbing system. Plumbing evaluations include inspection of accessible water lines, drain lines, and gas piping. Plumbing fixtures such as water heaters, sinks, toilets, tubs, showers, various faucets, and other related hardware are operated and inspected for damage, wear, improper installation, malfunction, leakage, and compliance with common safety standards. Some inspectors include landscape irrigation systems; some do not. Fire sprinkler systems are not tested, as this would cause severe moisture damage to the interior of the building.

Melted insulation indicates over-heated power supply connection in main panel. This is a fire hazard.

Ill-advised drain repair, courtesy of homeowner.

ASK THE INSPECTOR

Safety Device May Interfere with Safety

Dear Barry,

The GFCI outlet in my garage is wired to the automatic door opener and the fire sprinkler alarm. If the GFCI is tripped, the door and the fire alarm are both disabled. Do you think it's safe to wire these fixtures to the GFCI, or should we have the wiring changed?

Charles

Dear Charles,

Ground faulty circuit interrupters (GFCI) are required for electrical outlets in locations that are subject to possible moisture exposure. These include most outlets in garages. The purpose of GFCI outlets is to prevent injury or death resulting from electrical shock. They accomplish this by disconnecting the electrical power when there is an electrical imbalance in the circuit. Other locations requiring GFCI protection are bathrooms, kitchens, the exterior, pools, spas, wet bars, and laundry sinks.

The National Electrical Code does not specifically forbid GFCI protection for circuits that include garage door openers or fire alarms, but such installations are certainly impractical and could jeopardize the safety of occupants. In the event of a fire, water from the sprinklers could cause the GFCI to trip, rendering the alarm inoperative. In addition, lack of power to the garage door opener could inhibit emergency escape by persons in the building. My advice is to have these fixtures rewired.

ASK THE INSPECTOR

Toilet Repairs Left Me Flushed

Dear Barry,

When I bought my house, I hired a home inspector but was unable to attend the inspection. The report I received described water stains on the floor near the toilet and recommended installing a new "donut." When I asked the clerk at the local hardware store for a donut to fix my toilet, he looked at me as if I were some kind of nut myself. I expected him to direct me to the bakery down the street. Perhaps I didn't understand the inspection report. Is there such a thing as a donut that relates to toilet hardware?

Darnell

Dear Darnell,

You should have called your home inspector for a verbal review of the report. It would also be advisable to delegate toilet repairs to a licensed plumber, rather than seeking hardware supplies on your own.

A donut in the context of plumbing hardware is not something to be enjoyed with a cup of coffee. It is a ring of beeswax, approximately 5" in diameter, specifically used to seal the base of a toilet to the sewer pipe fitting at the floor. This essential plumbing component prevents leakage at the base of the toilet bowl. Although formally known as a wax ring seal, it is a "donut" in the general lexicon of construction jargon, as referenced by those who commonly wear their pants conspicuously below the belt line.

The darkened vinyl around your toilet is evidence of moisture below the surface. Replacing the seal will prevent further darkening, but the original color of the vinyl cannot be restored.

If your home is built on a concrete slab, moisture damage to the floor is likely to be cosmetic only. If you have a raised wood floor, consequential damage may include rotted framing and subfloor members. If that is the case, further evaluation by a licensed pest control operator is advised.

To replace the seal, the toilet should be drained and then lifted from the floor. The old seal should be scraped from the toilet base and the drain pipe before applying the new wax ring. Precise alignment is important when reinstalling the fixture, and tightening of the bolts should be done with care. Loose bolts can result in further leakage, while overtightening can cause the toilet base to crack.

It should be clear from these instructions that this is not a job for the uninitiated. To ensure that repairs are done correctly, let a professional do the work while you relax with a cup of coffee and a real donut.

Heating and cooling systems. Evaluation of temperature control systems includes inspection of the primary fixtures and the appurtenant equipment (such as ducts, piping, and fuel supply) to determine operability, wear, damage, faulty installation, and compliance with common safety standards.

Seller expects home inspector to forego evaluation of existing system. Silly boy!

Built-in appliances. Various appliances are excluded by some home inspectors, so check the contract and report to see which are included in the inspection. In general, most inspectors check the kitchen range and hood, dishwasher, garbage disposal, trash compactor, and possibly the microwave oven. Inspection of these fixtures is not exhaustive and is simply intended as an overview to determine general basic function, physical condition, and compliance with common safety standards. In-depth evaluation of these fixtures should be referred to appliance repair technicians.

Windows and doors. All doors and windows are checked for operability, installation, damage, wear, and evidence of moisture-related problems. Some inspectors check all doors and windows; others test only a representative number. The inspection report should indicate if not all doors and windows were tested.

Someone forgot to fasten the dishwasher to the cabinet. When the door is open, the fixture tips forward.

Window is poorly sealed. Evidence of repeated caulking indicates history of leakage.

ASK THE INSPECTOR

Spaced Out over Deck Spaces

Dear Barry,

Our deck is about 25 years old and has 12-inch-wide openings in the guardrails. Now that we're selling the property, the buyers' home inspector recommends smaller spaces to comply with current building codes. According to our neighbor, a licensed contractor, the railings were built to code at the time of construction and are therefore not subject to mandatory change. Is he right, or do we need to alter the rail spaces?

Glenda

Dear Glenda,

   Requirements affecting safety railings have undergone a gradual evolution in recent years. Prior to 1979, guardrail spacing was entirely unregulated. Then the first standards became effective, with the enactment of a nine-inch space limitation. In 1985, allowable openings were reduced to six inches; and in 1993 a maximum spacing of four inches became the current rule.

   The reason for these changes was to ensure that small children would be less likely to slip through the openings around high decks. Why these code changes were made in gradual increments, rather than with one logical adjustment to a child-proof size, is a challenge to common sense, but typical of bureaucratic thought processes.

   As to your current obligations as a seller, there is no requirement to upgrade older railing systems. If the buyers prefer compliance with current standards, upgrades should be performed at their expense, after the sale. But regardless of who pays for the improvements, the value of child safety clearly outweighs the issue of strict code compliance. If the height of your deck poses a significant hazard, modification of the railings is strongly advised, notwithstanding the age of the building or the codes that may apply.

Decks and balconies. Adjoining structures, such as decks and balconies, are checked for damage, wear, faulty construction, moisture-related problems, and unsafe conditions (usually involving substandard railings).

Poor drainage on balcony may promote leakage.

Ventilation. Rooms are checked to determine that adequate exterior ventilation is provided in accordance with accepted building and safety practices. This is particularly important for bathrooms and bedrooms.

Pavement. Paved surfaces are checked for general physical condition, direction of drainage, and possible trip hazards.

Fencing. Fences and gates in the general vicinity of the dwelling are checked for damage, wear, and operability. Many inspectors, however, specifically exclude fencing from their inspections.

CONDITIONS OUTSIDE THE SCOPE OF A HOME INSPECTION

Items typically excluded from a visual home inspection are as follows:

Code violations. This is an area where home inspectors walk on eggs. Industry standards specifically list building code compliance as not within the scope of a home inspection. This is because the building code, plumbing code, electrical code, mechanical code, fire code, and other related codes are encyclopedic in size and scope. No person could possibly master the entirety of these volumes, and expectations of that magnitude would subject home inspectors to unacceptable levels of liability. On the other hand, many of the faulty conditions routinely reported by home inspectors are specifically based upon standards set forth in the building code. If a home inspector says the risers in a staircase are 9 inches high and should not exceed 7¾ inches, where do these numbers originate? You guessed it: the building code. If a home inspector says the fire door in the garage must be self-closing, what is the source of that standard? Right again: the building code. "But I thought you said home inspectors don't do code compliance inspections." Well . . . to a limited extent they do, but don't tell them I said so. The problem here is that no one can accurately define the boundaries whereby the building code is applied to the home inspection process. Thus, home inspections should not be regarded as all-encompassing code compliance evaluations, even though the building code is applied in some cases (without the word *code* being specifically mentioned in the home inspection report).

The building code defines itself as a "minimum standard." Home inspectors are not code enforcement officers, but they have learned to use applicable portions of the code as guidelines for meaningful inspections. If all of this is not sufficiently clear to you, don't feel left out: it's not yet clear to everyone in the home inspection profession either.

ASK THE INSPECTOR

Buyer Concerned about Bats in Attic

Dear Barry,

We bought a home nearly a year ago and recently discovered bats in the attic. An exterminator quoted $1,000 to eliminate the pests and seal all the attic openings.

He also saw evidence that someone had previously tried to get rid of the bats, which means that the previous owner may have known about the problem but failed to disclose it to us. Furthermore, our home inspector went into the attic but said nothing about bats. Can we hold the seller or the home inspector liable for the costs of extermination?

Karl

Dear Karl,

In this case, the sellers and the home inspector may all be clear of disclosure liability. The sellers were required to disclose known defects prior to closing escrow. However, it is possible they believed the bat problem had been resolved.

As for the home inspector, discovery of vermin is not included within the standards of practice of the home inspection profession. Therefore, the inspector cannot be held liable for failure to disclose bats in the attic (or even the belfry), especially if this kind of problem was disclaimed in the inspection contract.

On the other hand, some home inspectors do report such conditions, even though they are not required to do so. The odor of bat residue can be intense, making detection almost unavoidable if the critters have been in the building for long. You can try to pursue the matter, but the chances of prevailing are probably slim.

Zoning violations. Zoning requirements vary from one neighborhood to the next and involve such considerations as building setbacks from property lines, building height limitations, flood zone designations, the number and type of units that can be constructed on a particular lot, and much more. Such conditions are definitely not within the scope of a home inspection. Further exclusions contained under this heading are:

- Building permit searches
- Recorded easements
- Rights of way
- Property boundaries
- Previous use of property
- Occupancy designation

Some home inspectors will investigate some of the foregoing conditions for additional fees. Otherwise, buyers can do their own research by checking with the local building department (for permits, a designation of legal use, or a history of past use), by reading the preliminary title report (for easements and rights of way), or by hiring a surveyor (to determine boundaries).

Condition of title. This information is outside the scope of a home inspection but is routinely disclosed in the preliminary title report, issued by the title insurance company prior to close of the transaction.

Third-party disclosures. Home inspectors are responsible for conditions that can be learned by way of inspection, not by interviewing owners, occupants, contractors, agents, neighbors, tenants, the girl next door, or any other persons. Of course, any pertinent information that is offered by persons in attendance should be pursued and verified as part of the routine inspection process. The inspector is there to discover as much as possible about the condition of the property, and detectives always appreciate a good lead from an informant.

Concealed conditions. Home inspectors are remarkably similar to normal people with respect to their inherent inability to see that which is not observable. In solemn acknowledgment of this lamentable handicap, home inspectors must disclaim liability for property defects that are located below ground, under slab floors, beneath insulation, within walls, behind personal property, inside fixtures and appliances, or not fully exposed and readily accessible for

A full inspection of this garage is simply not possible and should not be expected under these conditions.

any reason whatever, at the time of the inspection. Unfortunately, not everyone regards this as a reasonable exclusion.

ASK THE INSPECTOR

Are Home Inspectors Liable for Concealed Defects?

Dear Barry,

If I understand correctly, home inspectors are not permitted to open up walls, floors, or ceilings, or even to remove carpets. Doesn't this pose a liability problem for the inspector? As a remodeling contractor, I often find hidden problems when walls are opened. How do home inspectors stay out of trouble when concealed conditions are discovered after the sale?

Geoff

Dear Geoff,

Hidden defects often pose liability problems for home inspectors. In fact, countless lawsuits have been filed against inspectors for problems that were neither visible nor discernible at the time of the inspection. Inspection contracts and reports typically emphasize the fact that inspections are visual and do not involve exploratory surgery of concealed portions of the construction. Unfortunately, these disclaimers do not deter assertive tort attorneys from actively plying their trade, and this has been the bane of the home inspection profession since its inception.

The standard limitations of a home inspection are reasonable and logical: a home inspector is not permitted to dismantle portions of a seller's property. How could it be otherwise? If walls, ceilings, or floors were to be opened during an inspection, who would pay for all of the demolition and repairs? If destructive intrusion were allowed as part of the inspection process, how far would such demolition extend? Would inspectors merely spot-check a random sampling of concealed spaces or fully strip the drywall from the building to enable a total and complete evaluation of the framing, plumbing, electrical, and mechanical systems? After all, who knows where the hidden defects would finally be found? We might as well check everything.

Obviously, there are sane, sensible limits to a home inspection. When properly conducted by a competent, experienced professional, very few significant defects slip through the dragnet of the inspection process. Exceptions, of course, do occur, but until home inspectors develop X-ray vision, nonintrusive evaluation will be the defining limitation of the overall process. As to inspector liability, all that can be done is to state and restate inspection limitations within the text of the report and contract. For reasonable people, this will be acceptable; for others, ambulance chasers are standing in line to provide their services.

Determining fire resistance. This exclusion applies mainly to firewalls, such as in garages. To determine adequacy, the inspector would need to know the thickness and type of the drywall. In many cases, this cannot be determined without cutting holes in the material, and that would not be acceptable to sellers. In some cases, the thickness of the drywall can be determined by removing a cover plate from a wall outlet or light switch, but the question of fire rating would remain unanswered. If the garage ceiling is part of the firewall system, the inspector may be able to read the labeling on the drywall from within the garage attic.

Determining the fire rating of a door between a garage and a dwelling is also not always possible. In many cases, the installer of a fire door will remove the fire-rating tag, preventing future confirmation of the fire-resistant designation.

Common areas. At properties with collective ownership maintenance arrangements, such as condominiums, townhouses, and planned unit developments, home inspectors inspect only those areas of the property that are specific to the dwelling being purchased by the client. Some inspectors inspect only the interior portions of such properties, but this is an overreaching omission. Although the owners' association may be responsible for exterior repairs, it is still in the buyer's financial interest to be informed of exterior problems. For example, a deteriorated roof could result in water damage to the interior of the dwelling; substandard entry stairs could produce an injury lawsuit against the individual condo owner, as well as against the homeowners association; or faulty ground drainage problems could cause rot or mold to occur within the structure. Excluded common areas should be limited to those locations that do not directly affect the unit being inspected.

ASK THE INSPECTOR

Condo Owner at Odds with Home Inspector

Dear Barry,

I'm selling my condo and am annoyed with the buyer's home inspector. He insists on inspecting the exterior of the property, even though the outside of a condo is maintained by the owners' association and is not included in the sale. As far as I'm concerned, the exterior has nothing to do with this transaction. Why should the common areas be included in a home inspection?

Geoff

Dear Geoff,

There are conflicting schools of thought regarding which portions of a condominium should be included in a home inspection. Some inspectors evaluate the interior only, while others also inspect the immediate exterior. The argument against outside inspection is that the exterior is owned collectively by the owners' association and is not being purchased by the individual condo buyer.

The opposing view regards the exclusion of an outside inspection as a risky and overreaching omission. Although the owners' association may be responsible for exterior repairs, it is still in the buyer's financial interest to be informed of exterior problems. For example, a faulty chimney cap could cause a roof fire, or trees too close to the building could lead to foundation damage.

Considering the direct impact exterior problems can have on the interests of individual condominium owners and in view of the fact that each owner shares in the collective costs of the association, an exterior inspection is a reasonable part of a thorough condominium inspection.

Infestation. Conditions involving infestation by wood-destroying organisms such as termites, fungus, wood boring beetles, and the like are outside the scope of a home inspection. Furthermore, in most states it is illegal for anyone who is not a licensed pest control operator to make any disclosures regarding the presence of such organisms. Such disclosures by a home inspector would constitute a violation of the law in many (but not all) states. Disclosure of rodents is also prohibited in many states, as one must be a licensed exterminator to provide this type of information.

These are the uninvited guests who eat you out of house and home. Home inspectors call them insects. Pest control operators call them termites.

Some inspectors, however, get around these prohibitions by disclosing the problem without naming any specific type of infestation. For example, an inspector who notices obvious termite damage in an attic may disclose "possible insect damage," with a recommendation for further evaluation by a licensed pest control operator. Because the inspector has disclosed "insects" rather than "termites," the eternal wrath of the state disclosure police has been effectively appeased.

ASK THE INSPECTOR

Buyers Should Have Notified Home Inspector

Dear Barry,

Before buying our home, we hired an inspector. Unfortunately, he failed to disclose the termites in our attic. Instead, they were discovered by our handyman after we moved in, and we had to pay an exterminator. Do we have recourse against the inspector?

Larry

Dear Larry,

In most states, home inspections and termite inspections are separate processes, performed by different inspectors. If infestation was not included in the home inspection, a termite report should have been provided by a licensed pest control operator. On the other hand, if your home inspector included termite inspection as part of his service, then he would be liable if infestation was missed. However, the extermination that was performed after the inspection could change the liability aspect of the situation. Prior to correcting the termite problem, you should have called your inspector to review the infestation. Now that the evidence has been altered, it can no longer be proved that your inspector was at fault, and this may void any liability he may have had.

Engineering analysis. Evaluations regarding any type of engineering (structural, geotechnical, hydrological, etc.) are totally beyond the scope of a home inspection. For this type of information, buyers should engage the services of duly licensed engineers. A competent home inspector will recommend consulting a licensed engineer when defects warranting such evaluations are observed.

Technically complex equipment. Examples of equipment that would exceed the scope of a home inspection are remote control units, motion sensing and photoelectric devices, alarm systems, fire detection systems (other than smoke alarms), solar equipment, air-quality control systems, radio- or computer-controlled devices, automatic timer controls, elevators, dumbwaiters, satellite dishes, automatic gates, and so on.

Low-voltage electrical systems. Examples of low-voltage systems that would exceed the scope of a home inspection are TV antennae, cable TV systems, telephone systems, high-speed Internet systems, intercoms, security systems, speaker wires, automated equipment, landscape lighting, and so on.

Unattached appliances. As noted earlier, home inspections include most built-in appliances. Freestanding appliances, however, are typically not included as part of a property sale and, therefore, are typically not included in a home inspection. Common exclusions would be washers, dryers, refrigerators, countertop microwave ovens, portable dishwashers, and so on.

Noise transmission in multidwelling buildings. A common problem with some condominium dwellings is the lack of adequate soundproofing between adjoining units. In the course of a home inspection, it is not possible to ensure that walls and ceilings are sufficiently soundproofed unless the neighbors stage a raucous cacophony for the benefit of the inspector.

Environmental health hazards. Some home inspectors perform environmental hazard inspections as an additional service, but for most inspectors these are outside the scope of their normal services. Examples of such hazards include, among others, asbestos, formaldehyde, radon gas, lead paint, surface and airborne molds, and electromagnetic fields. However, with commonly recognized asbestos-containing materials, such as "cottage cheese ceilings," the prudent inspector will advise buyers that the material "may contain asbestos." Likewise, where mold stains are apparent or where musty odors are present, a competent inspector will recommend further evaluation by a mold specialist.

ASK THE INSPECTOR

Concerned about "Cottage Cheese Ceilings"

Dear Barry,

When we bought our house, it had what are commonly called "cottage cheese ceilings," and nobody mentioned at the time that this material could contain asbestos. We learned about this much later. Shouldn't somebody have disclosed this—either the seller, the agent, or the home inspector?

Arthur

Dear Arthur,

In spite of numerous published articles, many homeowners remain unaware that the textured ceilings in their homes might contain asbestos. Therefore, it is common for sellers to omit this disclosure in a real estate transaction.

Real estate professionals, on the other hand, have been exposed to so much asbestos-related information in trade journals, educational seminars, notices from Realtor associations, and common discussions within the industry that it's hard to imagine any agent or broker being unaware of ceiling texture as a potential vehicle for asbestos.

Among home inspectors, the likelihood of asbestos content in older ceiling texture is universal information, but disclosure of environmental hazards is typically not included in a professional home inspection. On the other hand, many inspectors inform clients that older acoustic-sprayed ceilings are likely to contain asbestos and routinely recommend further evaluation by a qualified expert. An omission of this kind is indicative of a marginal-quality home inspection, but the inspector would not be legally liable for this oversight if the inspection report listed asbestos as "not within the scope of the inspection."

On a positive note, asbestos-textured ceilings are not regarded as a significant health hazard if the material is undamaged and is left alone. Textured ceilings do not spontaneously emit asbestos fibers. The air can only become contaminated with asbestos fibers if the material is scraped or improperly removed. If the surface has been painted, then the asbestos is encapsulated and far safer than in its original form.

Many property owners are currently opting to remove textured ceilings as a means of updating the appearance of their homes. Before commencing such action, the textured material should be sampled and tested to determine if asbestos is present. If the test proves positive, removal and handling should be performed by a licensed asbestos abatement contractor.

The manufacture of asbestos-containing ceiling texture was banned in 1978, but this does not ensure that ceilings in newer homes do not contain asbestos. The installation of existing inventories was allowed after 1978 to prevent financial loss to those who had produced or purchased this material. Therefore, it is not uncommon to find asbestos in textured ceilings installed in the 1980s.

Private water systems. In most areas of the country, private water supply systems, such as wells and water purifiers, are not within the scope of a home inspection. Whenever a home with a water well is being purchased, the seller should hire a licensed well contractor to perform a complete well test and provide a report of the findings. Water purification systems and water softeners should be evaluated by technicians in the business of installing and servicing such equipment.

Well systems should be tested by qualified well contractors.

Private sewage systems. Evaluation of septic systems is not within the scope of a home inspection in most areas of the country. Whenever a home with a septic system is being purchased, the seller should hire a licensed septic contractor to excavate, pump, and inspect the system, and to provide a report of the findings. Sewage ejector pumps are also beyond the scope of a home inspection and should be evaluated by a licensed plumber familiar with this type of equipment.

In some areas of the country, however, home inspectors are known to include septic systems as part of a home inspection. Prudent buyers should beware of such services: Unless a septic inspection includes evacuation of the tank (a process requiring the use of a specialized pump truck), such inspections should be regarded with a generous dose of suspicion. Without emptying the tank and inspecting its interior, an adequate evaluation is not possible.

Most home inspectors exclude sewage ejector systems, deferring them to the expertise of licensed plumbers.

ASK THE INSPECTOR

Are Septic Tanks Included in a Home Inspection?

Dear Barry,

We purchased a home in the country and hired a home inspector to find the defects. After moving in, we had a major sewage backup. The septic contractor said the system is substandard, and replacement is estimated at $5,000. We think the *home inspector should have found this problem, but he says that septic systems are not included in a home inspection. Why was something so basic omitted?*

Wayne

Dear Wayne,

Disputes over home inspections often involve misunderstandings about the scope of the inspection process. To avoid disagreements, it is important to read every word of the inspector's report. Most inspection contracts specifically outline the scope of the inspection and list common limitations.

Home inspections are basically defined as visual inspections only, which means that the inspector evaluates conditions that are exposed to view. Property components concealed within the construction, below ground, or in other inaccessible areas are not included. This limitation directly affects septic systems because they are totally buried and must be excavated to enable proper evaluation.

Even after excavation, septic systems require far more than visual inspection. To determine quality and condition, the tank must be drained and the leach field tested. This can only be done by a contractor in the business of servicing and maintaining private sewage systems.

Septic systems are complex in nature, requiring specialized knowledge and equipment to provide competent diagnosis. Basically, they are sewage treatment plants in miniature and require expertise well beyond that of a home inspector.

In most sales transactions, the seller pays for a septic inspection and report. Apparently, no one advised you to request this service from your seller. Purchasing rural property without a professional septic inspection is a gamble and can have costly results. When a septic stops working, the only thing that goes down the drain is money.

Swimming pools and hot tubs. In areas of the country with many swimming pools, it is a standard practice for home inspectors to include a pool inspection, although this is often done for an additional fee. In areas with fewer pools, home inspectors have less opportunity to become familiar with the many types of pool equipment on the market and the intricacies of pool systems in general. These home inspectors typically exclude pools and hot tubs from their inspections. The alternative for homebuyers is to hire a qualified pool contractor to perform that part of the inspection.

Related equipment that is generally excluded from a home inspection includes:

- Waterfalls

- Ponds

- Fountains

- Saunas

- Steam baths

Value appraisal. Price valuation is not within the scope of a home inspection. Unless the property is being purchased with cash, the mortgage lender will provide, or require, the services of an appraiser. This is the person with the expertise to determine the correct market value of the property.

Measurements of buildings or property. The purpose of a home inspection is to determine quality, not quantity. Some home inspectors may do measurements for an additional fee, but this is generally not within the scope of a home inspection. Square-footage measurements are usually provided by the loan appraiser.

Estimated repair costs. For most home inspectors, estimates of repair costs are excluded. Some home inspectors provide cost estimates as an additional service, usually for an additional fee, but these estimates commonly provide a broad range of possible costs for each repair, rather than a specific amount.

Note: Buyers should beware of home inspectors who provide the estimate and then offer to do the work. It is a conflict of interest for home inspectors to perform work on homes they inspect. Furthermore, it violates the codes of ethics of all home inspector associations and is illegal in some states.

ASK THE INSPECTOR

Buyer Wants Repair Cost Estimates

Dear Barry,

After spending $300 for a home inspection and getting a long list of problems, the inspector wouldn't tell me the total cost to repair everything he had found.

What's the point of a home inspection if I don't know how much money is needed to address the defects?

Bill

Dear Bill,

Some home inspectors provide cost estimates with their inspections, but most do not. Furthermore, those who do provide estimates typically charge an additional fee to compensate for the time needed to prepare the figures.

The main problem with repair cost estimates offered by home inspectors is that they are usually very rough guesstimates, rather than accurate computations. Home inspectors who provide these numbers usually give a broad range of potential costs. For example, a roof repair estimate might be stated as "between $3,000 and $5,000."

Rather than relying on vague cost projections, you should take your home inspector's list of property defects and obtain specific repair bids from licensed contractors. Not only will you have an accurate idea of costs, but you will have definite commitments to those numbers.

Electrical load calculation. This is an esoteric electrical evaluation, routinely performed by electrical contractors, and is well outside the scope of a standard home inspection. It involves mathematical computations whereby the size and number of circuits in the electrical system are measured against the overall capacity of the service—the purpose being to determine whether a higher-rated electric service is needed.

Latent defects. Home inspectors are neither prophets nor fortune tellers, and therefore cannot predict how long a particular property component will continue to function. Systems that are fully operative at the time of inspection can fail unexpectedly, and they can do so shortly after the close of the transaction. In most cases, it is simply not possible to foretell sudden failure or to estimate how long a component will continue to operate. Such predictions are beyond the scope of a home inspection. For further information in this regard, tea leaves should be consulted.

Testing gas shutoff valves. Home inspectors do not test gas shutoff valves because this would entail the reigniting of pilot lights after such tests. However, most gas companies provide free safety evaluations of gas fixtures upon request. It is recommended that this be done prior to closing the sale.

Unusual gas and electric fixtures. Exterior fixtures, such as patio heaters, barbecues, saunas, and fire pits, are likely to be excluded by most home inspectors.

Detached ancillary buildings. The basic home inspection fee typically covers the dwelling and garage. Additional structures, such as barns, shops, extra garages, or additional living units, will usually be excluded except for an additional inspection fee.

Advisability of purchase. Home inspectors are consultants regarding the physical condition of property. They are not financial or investment counselors. A buyer's decision to complete a transaction is a personal one, based upon many factors that are beyond the professional expertise of a home inspector. A property that is a good investment for one person might not be a wise purchase for someone else. A property defect that is a deal killer for one buyer may not be a decisive issue to another. Buyers who seek counsel regarding the practicality of completing a purchase should consult an accountant or investment advisor.

Requirements of Americans with Disabilities Act (ADA). ADA requirements are complicated and convoluted—a testament to the needless complexities of the intractable bureaucratic mind. Furthermore, they do not apply to most residential properties. Very few inspectors are sufficiently versed in these requirements, and those who possess this knowledge usually perform ADA inspections on commercial properties as a separate service for an additional fee.

Cosmetic finishes. Home inspectors generally report on cosmetic defects as a courtesy only, as the purpose of the inspection is to report "significant" defects. Cosmetic defects likely to be reported include weathered exterior siding or peeling paint.

Landscaping. Home inspectors generally report on landscape defects as a courtesy only. Exceptions to this exclusion would be trees, vines, and other plants that adversely affect buildings or other structures on the property.

Tree roots this close to foundation can damage structure.

Fire sprinklers. There is no way to test a fire sprinkler system without causing major water damage to the interior of the building. Fire sprinklers must be taken on faith unless evaluated by a licensed plumbing contractor with expertise in the installation and repair of such systems.

ASK THE INSPECTOR

Palm Tree Roots Damage Garage

Dear Barry,

We bought our home several months ago. Recently, while cleaning our garage, we moved a cabinet and found that roots from our neighbors' palm tree had broken through the stucco wall and the cement foundation. The tree was removed a few months ago, but the stump was left in place, possibly because it had become part of our garage. Neither the seller nor our home inspector disclosed this condition when we bought the property. Should the stump be removed to prevent termite problems, and who is responsible for the repairs?

Jillian

Dear Jillian,

Structural damages often occur when trees with the potential for significant growth are thoughtlessly planted adjacent to buildings. In response to your two questions, I offer the following four answers:

1. *It would be wise to have the tree stump removed, as you suggested, to prevent termite infestation.*
2. *It is possible that your homeowners insurance may cover damages caused by tree roots, but the insurer may disclaim this as a preexisting condition. You'll have to check with your insurance agent.*

3. *It is possible that the owner of the late tree may bear some responsibility for the damages to your property, but this is a question for an attorney rather than a home inspector.*

4. *As to disclosure liability: (a) The inspector who checked your home prior to purchase may be off the hook for not observing a concealed defect within the garage, but there remains the question of why he failed to observe the tree damage at the exterior of the building; and (b) it would seem reasonable to expect that the sellers of the property were aware of the problem, as it must have taken years for the damages to fully develop. If they were aware of the root intrusion and the resultant effects to the building, they had a legal obligation to disclose this to you. Failure to do so may constitute a violation of your state's disclosure laws.*

Landscape sprinklers. Some home inspectors test yard sprinklers but some do not. This is a professional choice made by each inspection company. Most sprinkler systems are installed by homeowners rather than contractors, and most have idiosyncracies familiar only to the owner or the gardener. Therefore, it is wise to have the owner or gardener provide a demonstration of the system to prospective buyers.

Technically exhaustive inspections. Home inspectors do not perform dismantling or technical testing of equipment. Systems are operated and observed to determine apparent defects. More complex types of testing typically require the services of specialized contractors or technicians.

Product recalls. Most home inspectors do not provide product recall information because it would be too difficult to stay current on the numerous plumbing, electrical, mechanical, and general construction products continually being recalled by manufacturers.

The foregoing standards and limitations provide homebuyers with a realistic framework for understanding their home inspection and, it is hoped, will prevent needless disagreements from occurring if property defects are discovered after the sale.

CHAPTER SEVEN

The Home Inspector's Liability

There are two kinds of home inspectors: those who have been sued and those who will be.

CONVERGING VIEWS OF LIABILITY

Financial liability is a central, critical consideration for all members of the home inspection profession. It is the fearsome "monster under the bed" in the life of every home inspector. All inspectors, from time to time, must address problems that were not disclosed in an inspection report but were discovered after the close of the sale. In some of these cases, conflicts arise as to who bears liability: the seller, the agent, the home inspector, some contractor or tradesperson who performed faulty work, or various combinations of all these people. Conflicts of this kind can generally be viewed from four colliding perspectives: that of the buyer, the seller, the real estate agent, and, of course, the home inspector.

The Buyer's Perspective

Homebuyers rely on their inspector's ability to discover and report defects. They base a major financial decision upon that reliance. If undisclosed problems are discovered after the sale, the inspector is presumed to have failed in his professional duties and may be pressed to pay for necessary repairs. Sometimes the demands of buyers are valid, based solidly upon inspector negligence; at such times, inspector liability is a reasonable expectation. At other times, a buyer's claims may involve defects that were not apparent at the time of the inspection or not within the defined scope of the inspection; this is when liability expectations exceed reasonable boundaries. Unfortunately, in the mind's eye of some buyers, the inspector may be viewed as an unconditional insurance company—no deductible, no exclusions. All too often, undue pressures are directed against the inspector and emphasized through the paid efforts of legal hired guns (commonly known as attorneys). Common sense and fairness are needed when these situations occur, but those qualities are not predominant in the practice of tort law. Therefore, buyers are strongly advised to maintain reasonable, fair-minded perspectives regarding such issues.

ASK THE INSPECTOR

Inspector Did Not Inspect the Subarea

Dear Barry,

A few months ago, I purchased my first home and hired a home inspector to check it out. I was with him for the entire inspection, and he never once went under the house. At the time, I didn't think about it, but since then a plumber discovered leaking sewage under the bathroom. The seller and I shared the repair costs, but I think the inspector should reimburse us. Can you tell me if he is liable?

Jeremy

Dear Jeremy,

Whether the home inspector is liable depends on several considerations: the laws in your state, the wording of the inspection contract, the inspector's reasons for not inspecting the subarea, and the standards of practice indicated in the report.

Most home inspectors base their work upon the standards of practice of the American Society of Home Inspectors or an equivalent organization. All such standards include a crawl through the subarea as part of an acceptable home inspection. So many significant conditions are considered during that part of the inspection that the final report cannot be regarded as thorough or complete unless the subarea has been evaluated.

Without crawling beneath the building, it is not possible to adequately assess the foundation system, the floor framing, ground drainage, electrical wiring, water piping, drain lines, gas pipes, portions of the heating system, etc. Bypassing that part of the inspection, unless access was not possible, constitutes professional negligence, particularly if the inspection report did not indicate that this part of the building was not inspected.

However, without knowing the inspector's reasons for not entering the subarea, judgment should be withheld. The inspector should be contacted and afforded the opportunity to respond to your complaint.

The Agent's Perspective

Real estate agents view the inspector as a medium of liability reduction and are encouraged by their attorneys and by professional real estate associations to emphasize this aspect of the inspector-agent relationship. Part of the problem here is the pressure that is placed upon agents to disclose conditions not within their area of expertise. In many states, agents must perform visual walk-through inspections, providing written disclosure of observed problems. This is a difficult position for many agents, pressed as they are to perform disclosure functions for which they are not professionally qualified. Home inspectors provide agents with some of the stopgap protection they need, significantly reducing the numbers of undisclosed defects, while at the same time assuming a portion of the liability in the event of discoveries after the sale. In some states, lobbyists representing real estate associations have promoted legislation designed to shift more liability away from agents and onto home inspectors. Such legislation is obviously biased toward special interest concerns, rather than benefiting the home-buying public.

ASK THE INSPECTOR

Home Inspector Damaged My Gutters

Dear Barry,

As a Realtor, I do business with many home inspectors, but this one guy always makes problems for my sellers. Last week, he bent the rain gutter on one of my listings. I checked this out later by placing a ladder against the building and found that the gutters bend quite easily. Other workers have been on this roof, but they have never bent the gutters. What can home inspectors do to prevent this kind of problem?

Ron

Dear Ron,

Inspectors and other tradespeople should indeed take care not to adversely affect the condition of properties where they work. Unfortunately, not everyone takes this responsibility seriously.

With regard to your client's rain gutters, these typically consist of thin-gauge sheet metal that bends easily under the weight of an occupied ladder. Fortunately, there is a simple method for leaning heavy loads, such as ladders, against gutters without causing damage. The trick is to place the ladder so that its rails straddle one of the fasteners securing the gutters to the building. These points of attachment are the only places where the gutters are reinforced against lateral pressure. If the ladder is placed at the intermediate locations between these fasteners, bending is very likely to occur. Apparently, your inspector did not consider this.

The Seller's Perspective

In most states, sellers are required by law to disclose all property conditions that would be of interest or concern to a buyer, which means that all known defects should be disclosed in writing. In practice, the fulfillment of such a requirement depends largely upon what a seller actually knows about the condition of the property as well as the ethical inclinations of the individual seller. For those sellers who are morally predisposed to abridge the disclosure process, the home inspector is often viewed as a legal scapegoat. Instead of disclosing known defects at the outset of the transaction, the ethically challenged seller will play a game of wait and see—that is, let's withhold disclosure until we see what the home inspector finds. If the inspector misses a particular defect, the seller may then presume that the liability has been legally transferred. If undisclosed problems are realized after the sale, the seller simply says, "That's the home inspector's responsibility."

Again, common sense and fairness (and in this case legal compliance) are at issue. The home inspector was not hired to indemnify a dishonest seller. The inspector is a consultant to the buyers. The responsibility of sellers to disclose all known defects is a separate and distinct legal obligation having nothing whatsoever to do with the buyers' home inspection.

ASK THE INSPECTOR

This Home Inspector Must Be Blind

Dear Barry,

The home inspector who checked our house seems to need a thick pair of glasses. His report listed two electrical circuits as being "overfused." Our electric panel has circuit breakers, not fuses. How can a professional inspector make such an obvious and elementary mistake?

Pat

Dear Pat,

The term overfused *does not refer exclusively to fuses. It is a technical expression that applies to improper overload protection for an electrical circuit, regardless of whether there are circuit breakers or fuses in the service panel.*

The purpose of a circuit breaker or fuse is to disconnect the power in the event of an overload. For example, let's say that a particular wire is designed to carry 15 amps of electricity. If more than 15 amps are drawn through the wire, overheating will occur. A 15-amp fuse or circuit breaker would discontinue the flow of electricity if this were to happen. However, if we connect this 15-amp wire to a 20-amp circuit breaker or fuse, we have created the hazardous condition known as overfusing. Now if an overload takes place, the breaker or fuse will not trip until an excess of 20 amps of power is passing through the circuit. This means that the wire and insulation could overheat, causing a fire in the home. Fortunately, your home inspector's eyesight was adequate to identify this hazardous condition without the benefit of thick glasses.

The overfusing in your service panel should be corrected immediately. And be sure to have the work done by a licensed electrician, not a handyman or other type of contractor.

The Home Inspector's Perspective

Home inspectors are caught in the crossfire of conflicting concerns—the buyers' need to know, the agents' desire to avoid professional liability, and the inability or unwillingness of sellers to provide adequate disclosure. Thus, legal and financial exposure has become the universal bane of the home inspection profession. The greatest fear of every inspector is the ominous certified letter or summons demanding payment for some defect that was discovered after the sale. This is an aspect of the inspection business not adequately considered by entry-level inspectors but which all inspectors eventually come to appreciate through direct and inevitable experience.

Regardless of the demands and expectations of others, home inspectors should assume a reasonable degree of responsibility for the quality and consequences of their work. But no degree of talent or effort can prevent occasional mistakes. All inspectors make them, as do the practitioners of every profession. And as with all other professions, some assume higher levels of integrity and responsibility than others. Each home inspector must make choices regarding claims for unreported property defects; and these choices, it is hoped, will be based upon what is fair and honest, rather than what is comfortable and expedient.

ASK THE INSPECTOR

Home Inspector Troubled over Disputes

Dear Barry,

As a home inspector, I've had an angry complaint from a seller and am seeking clarification on two issues. First, my report discloses missing window screens. The seller disagrees with this disclosure because screens are not listed in the purchase contract as items to be repaired. The other problem involves distribution of the inspection report. The buyer who hired me wants to keep all copies of the report and refuses to share them with the seller or the agent. This puts me in the middle, but I feel bound to respect the wishes of the buyer. How do you view these conflicts?

Tony

Dear Tony,

Complaints and misunderstandings are common distractions for home inspectors, due in part to the relative newness of the home inspection business. In today's market, many sellers are having their first experiences with home inspection, and some are imposing their preconceived expectations on an unfamiliar process.

The responsibility of a home inspector is to the client—typically the buyer. This often involves sensitive issues, requiring patience and understanding by all parties in a transaction. Occasional misunderstandings are inevitable, calling for thoughtful, detailed explanations. Regarding your two questions, your general approach is reasonable and well-founded:

1. *It doesn't matter whether window screen replacement is contractual. Your job is to list all visible defects. The decision to repair, not to repair, or who should repair is a matter for negotiation between the parties in the transaction and is not the business or concern of the home inspector. The job of the inspector is to provide information, pure and simple, not to make contractual interpretations or to disclose only those problems the seller has agreed to repair.*

2. *All copies of the report are the property of the client—in most cases, the buyer. It is the client's choice whether to share these copies with others. In many cases, the purchase contract obligates the buyer to provide report copies to the seller. But again, interpretation and implementation of the contract is not the province of the home inspector. People may become angry with home inspectors when copies are not distributed, but the hands of inspectors are tied in this respect. All they can do is explain as politely as possible that they are legally bound to carry out the wishes of their clients. If the contract calls for report distribution, that is the responsibility of the client.*

FAIR AND UNFAIR LIABILITY

Stated as bluntly and succinctly as possible, fair liability occurs when a home inspector has screwed up in the course of an inspection. Unfair liability occurs when a home inspector has not screwed up in the course of an inspection and yet is being pursued. Both of these situations commonly occur.

Three sets of criteria define the circumstances for which home inspectors are rightfully and reasonably liable:

1. *Apparent defects missed by the inspector:* These are conditions that were visibly identifiable; that were not concealed in any significant way, and yet were not observed or reported by the inspector.

2. *Defects within the scope of the inspection:* These refer to conditions that are specified in the standards of practice of the various

national and state home inspector associations or are required by law in those states that license or regulate home inspectors.

3. *Damages caused by inspector carelessness:* Examples of damages resulting from carelessness are infinite. An inspector breaks a vase, damages a tile roof, forgets to turn off the oven, overflows a second-floor bathtub, cracks a window, turns off the power to the meat freezer, falls through the ceiling while inspecting the attic, lets the parrot fly out of the house.

These are situations and events when, as unpleasant as the consequences may be, home inspectors must step up to the plate and assume some level of responsibility. It is the painful acid test of integrity that most home inspectors, sooner or later, must face.

ASK THE INSPECTOR

Home Inspector Missed Major Plumbing Defect

Dear Barry,

We recently bought a home and thought we had gotten a thorough home inspection. The inspector told us that the old galvanized steel plumbing would soon need replacement but that it would be operative for at least another year. After moving in, we found that the dishwasher and sink faucet wouldn't work because the hot water line to the kitchen was completely congested with rust. Nothing was mentioned about this in the inspection report; in fact, the dishwasher was listed as functional. We believe our home inspector was negligent but don't know what to do about it.

Rick

Dear Rick,

Two aspects of this situation would appear to constitute negligence on the part of the home inspector. You say the inspector identified deteriorated water piping but that he advised continued use rather than a follow-up by a licensed plumber. This is not a typical recommendation for badly rusted water lines.

Home inspectors function as residential pathologists, providing preliminary diagnoses of faulty conditions. When symptoms of a significant plumbing defect are discovered, the standard recommendation is "further evaluation by a licensed plumber." An inspector who designates rusted water lines as "functional," without *advising further review, has made a judgment that is not consistent with industry standards and has undertaken a substantial level of liability.*

Next, there is the matter of no hot water at kitchen fixtures. Normal home inspection procedures would lead an inspector to discover the lack of hot water at a faucet. How this condition was missed is puzzling. Add to this the undisclosed absence of water at the dishwasher, and one must ask by what method the inspector deduced his findings. Typical evaluation of a dishwasher involves, among other things, filling the fixture with water, observing the wash cycle, and watching the unit drain. If no water was entering the washer, it is surprising that the unit passed muster.

Unfortunately, situations of this kind do not always have a positive remedy, and recourse against a home inspector can depend largely upon liability laws in a given state. Hopefully, the inspector is willing to work with you in addressing the matter. You should bring the matter to his attention and request that he reinspect the kitchen plumbing.

Unfortunately, there are also times when home inspectors are held to the fire for defects not defined by established standards and not observable at the time of inspection. Examples of unfair claims and frivolous litigation abound and include the following:

1. After purchasing a home, the buyer hires a contractor to remodel the house. The contractor opens some walls and finds plumbing or electrical problems that were not reported by the home inspector. The inspector could not possibly have found these defects, but to the buyer's attorney that is irrelevant and immaterial.

2. The home inspection occurs during dry summer weather. After the sale, winter rains cause flooding below the building, or leaking at the windows, or wetness inside the fireplace. The seller in this case had masked all symptoms of past water problems, preventing the home inspector from detecting these conditions. The inspector could not have known, but so what? Someone has to pay for waterproofing the house. It's not fair that the buyer should have to pay, so why not the inspector?

3. In most states, termite damage and dry rot can be reported only by a licensed pest control operator. Home inspectors in those states are specifically forbidden by law from making such dis-

closures. Nevertheless, many home inspectors have been sued when undisclosed infestation was discovered after the sale.

The legal dramas that proceed from such claims give rise to exhaustively detailed home inspection contracts, with fine print designed by attorneys to clarify which conditions are covered in a home inspection and which conditions are not. Before hiring a home inspector, buyers should read these contracts carefully to gain an accurate understanding of which services the inspector actually provides and which conditions are specifically excluded from the inspection process. The majority of such exclusions were described in Chapter 6.

ASK THE INSPECTOR

Rush to Judgment against Home Inspector

Dear Barry,

We're selling our home, and the buyer hired a home inspector who doesn't seem to know his business. He reported that our garage outlets lack ground fault protection. We called the electrician who wired our house, and he said the garage outlets were wired according to code. He even mailed us a letter certifying this fact in writing. It wasn't easy, but we finally convinced the buyer that the outlets are OK. How can sellers protect themselves from blatant mistakes by know-it-all home inspectors?

Bonnie

Dear Bonnie,

There is something about your circumstance that needs clarification. You say the home inspector reported a faulty electrical condition, and the problem was resolved by written assurances from an electrician? What I'm not hearing is the part about the electrician coming to your home and testing the garage outlets to ensure that they are truly equipped with ground fault protection. Unless your electrician is exempt from potential human error, he would do well to recheck his work just to be on the safe side.

The situation under debate involves electrical safety compliance. Rather than rushing to judgment against the home inspector, would it not be in everyone's best interests to physically evaluate the garage outlets and consider the slim possibility that the electrician might have made a mistake? Is it not even possible that one of *the ground fault devices installed at the time of construction became defective at a later date? Does it not make sense to test the outlets just to be sure they are OK?*

May I suggest a simple test that anyone can perform with or without electrical expertise? Each of the ground fault outlets in your home is equipped with a built-in test button. When the test button is pressed, the power to the circuit is interrupted. I recommend that you push each of these test buttons, thereby disconnecting all protected outlets. Once this is done, plug an appliance (a lamp, a radio, whatever) into each of the garage outlets. If these outlets still have power, then they lack ground fault protection and the electrician has some corrective work to perform.

In addition, the home inspector should be afforded the opportunity to defend the findings in his report. This inspector is no less prone to error than anyone else. But in all fairness, he should be given as much chance as the electrician to present his case. After all, the issue being disputed is not academic; it's a matter of personal safety.

ACTUAL MONETARY LIABILITY

The financial liability of home inspectors varies according to the laws of individual states. Inspection contracts often set specific dollar amounts as the limit of liability, but not all states recognize these contract provisions. In some states, laws allow inspectors to restrict their liability to a simple refund of the inspection fee, regardless of repair costs for undisclosed defects. In other states, judges routinely disallow such limitations and award plaintiffs large damage awards against home inspectors.

Some contracts limit liability to several times the inspection fee or to the amount of the deductible in the inspector's errors and omissions insurance policy. When a claim occurs, the inspector simply pays the deductible and lets the insurance company assume responsibility for the remaining costs or for legal defense.

These considerations underscore the recommendation stated in Chapter 4: Make sure your inspector is insured for errors and omissions.

Home inspector liability is discussed further in Chapter 9.

ASK THE INSPECTOR

Statute of Limitations on Home Inspection

Dear Barry,

    We bought our house about 12 years ago, and the home inspector at the time said the heating system was in good condition. Now we've learned that the warm-air ducts below the house are rotted and need to be replaced. Worse still, they are wrapped with asbestos, and removal will cost an extra $1,500. Shouldn't these problems have been reported by our home inspector?

Audrey

Dear Audrey,

    Your questions cover several distinct issues. To begin, let's clarify that warm-air ducts do not rot; they rust. Rot happens to organic materials such as wood. Apparently, ground moisture beneath your home has caused major rust damage to the metal ducts. In this regard, time is a major consideration. It's been more than a decade since your home was inspected, and that is more than enough time for rust damage to have occurred. It is entirely possible that the ducts were in good condition when you bought the home, which would account for the favorable report by the home inspector.

    On the other hand, air ducts below a house typically do not rust unless they are in continuous contact with wet soil or are exposed to condensation. If they are properly lifted and secured above the ground, and if the subarea is well vented, they should have been adequately protected from moisture. Apparently, there was a problem in that regard that should have been disclosed by your home inspector, even if there was no rust damage at the time.

    As to the asbestos insulation, disclosure of environmentally hazardous material, such as asbestos, is not within the scope of a home inspection. Nevertheless, a competent home inspector, acting as an advocate for the client, should mention to the client that suspect materials were observed. In that respect, the inspector could be faulted but would probably not bare legal liability.

    Finally, we should revisit the issue of elapsed time. Even if your inspector had been liable when you bought the house, the statute of limitations for professional negligence has probably expired. Notwithstanding other considerations, it would be very difficult to press the issue of liability at this late date.

CHAPTER EIGHT

After the Inspection: Repairs and Renegotiation

*Moving ahead, starting over,
or walking away.*

GUIDELINES FOR NEGOTIATION

Upon completion of a home inspection, the inspector reviews and explains all of the conditions and defects that were discovered. Buyers, at this point, are often uncertain what to do with the lengthy list of newly disclosed information and commonly ask: "Which items are the sellers required to repair?" and "What if the sellers won't address these problems?"

Home inspectors can provide guidelines and perspectives in answer to these questions, but most essential at this stage of the transaction is representation by an agent or broker with strong negotiating skills and a sense of commitment to the buyers' best interests. How matters are handled at this juncture can determine the degree of benefit buyers attain from the inspection and the level of satisfaction to be enjoyed when the sale is completed. Failure to properly apply the new disclosures can negate the purpose of the inspection.

The first point buyers must understand is that home inspection reports are not repair lists for sellers. The one exception to this rule applies to brand-new homes, where the builder or contractor must provide a finished product free of defects. With used homes, inspection reports provide information for buyers rather than directives for sellers. This does not mean that buyers cannot submit repair requests to sellers, but most such requests are negotiable, not legally binding upon the sellers. Repair requests can and should be made but with the understanding that most sellers have rights of refusal.

ASK THE INSPECTOR

Inspection Report Not a Repair List for Seller

Dear Barry,

We hired a home inspector to make a complete repair list for the home we are buying, but it seems that we wasted our money. The inspector did a thorough job and disclosed some serious plumbing and electrical problems. But the seller refused to fix anything. We thought that sellers must repair the problems discovered by home inspectors, but our agent says that most repairs are negotiable. This is all very disillusioning. If a seller has no obligation to make these repairs, then what's the point of having a home inspection?

Nancy

Dear Nancy,

Your question voices a common misunderstanding about the purpose of a home inspection. People often view an inspection report as a mandatory repair list for the seller. The fact is, sellers are not required to produce a flawless house. They have no such obligation by law or by contract, unless such an arrangement was agreed upon in advance.

As disappointing as this may seem, most repairs are subject to negotiation between the parties of a sale. Typically, buyers will ask that various conditions be repaired before the transaction is completed, and sellers will usually acquiesce to some of these requests. But with most building defects, sellers make repairs as a matter of choice, not obligation—to foster goodwill or to facilitate consummation of the sale. There are, of course, those few rigid sellers who flatly refuse to fix anything, even at the risk of losing the sale. Fortunately, this response is the exception rather than the rule.

Sellers maintain the legal right to refuse repair demands, except where requirements are set forth by state law, local ordinance, or the real estate purchase contract. Legal obligations include earthquake straps for water heaters (in areas where required) and smoke detectors in specified portions of the home. Some contracts stipulate that fixtures be in working condition at the close of the sale, that windows not be broken, and that there be no existing leaks in the roof or plumbing.

Before you make any demands of the seller, try to evaluate the inspection report with an eye toward problems of greatest significance. Look for conditions that compromise health and safety or involve active leakage. Most sellers will address problems affecting sensitive areas such as the roof, fireplace, gas-burning fixtures, or electrical wiring.

Routine maintenance items warrant a lesser degree of concern and should not be pressed upon the seller. If the house is not brand-new, it is unreasonable to insist boldly upon correction of all defects. Such demands can alienate the seller and kill the deal. Your willingness to accept minor problems may persuade a seller to correct conditions of greater substance.

The purpose of a home inspection is not to corner the seller with a repair list. The primary objective is to know what you are buying before you buy it. All homes have defects; it's not possible to acquire one that is perfect. What you want is a working knowledge of significant defects before you take possession. As the old sea captain once told me, "It doesn't matter if your boat has a leak, as long as you know it's leaking."

With this ground rule in place, buyers should divide the inspection findings into four distinct categories:

1. *Legally mandated repairs:* Some conditions require repairs in accordance with state laws or local ordinances. Common in many areas are requirements to provide water-conserving toilets and showerheads, to upgrade smoke detector placement, to strap water heaters in areas prone to earthquakes, or to comply with various building and safety standards. Such items are obviously nonnegotiable and must be addressed by the sellers.

2. *Contractually mandated repairs:* Some conditions are specified for repair in the real estate purchase contract. Typical among these are stipulations that all building components be in working condition, that broken windows be replaced, that plumbing leaks be repaired, or that the roof be certified by a licensed roofing contractor. Contractual agreements of this kind are binding upon sellers.

3. *Negotiable repairs:* All property defects not included in items 1 and 2 above are negotiable, and buyers should carefully divide these according to importance. Vital repairs, such as structural

problems or safety violations, although not incumbent upon sellers, are generally regarded as reasonable repair requests. Even though sellers are not obligated for such corrective work, most reasonable sellers agree to address conditions of this kind, either by making repairs or by adjusting the sales price of the property. Examples of such conditions include faulty foundations, a nonpermitted addition, a defective furnace, a substandard chimney, and faulty electrical wiring. Although sellers are not required to make these repairs, buyers should feel comfortable requesting that such corrections be completed.

4. *Conditions of minor concern:* Finally, there are those common property defects that should be regarded for disclosure purposes only and that buyers should accept as conditions to be repaired after the sale. Examples are numerous and include rotted fence posts, peeling paint, rubbing doors, cracked pavement, worn carpet, obsolete appliances, and the like.

ASK THE INSPECTOR

How to Negotiate After the Home Inspection

Dear Barry,

After a home inspection is completed, how should a buyer negotiate price adjustments and repairs into the deal? Do you have any tips?

Arlington

Dear Arlington,

When you receive a home inspection report, deciding what to do next can be perplexing and challenging. It is probably the touchiest transitional phase in the entire purchase process. The original haggling was hard enough: an agreement was made on the price and terms of the deal, and you thought everything was set. Now, suddenly, with new revelations posed by the home inspector, negotiations are reopened and nothing is certain.

The question, at this point, is: "What repair requests are appropriate?" As a general rule in most transactions, your negotiating position will depend upon the answers to the following five questions:

1. *What repairs are mandated by law?* In some states and municipalities, sellers are required to make specified upgrades. For example, smoke alarms

might have to comply with current building codes or plumbing fixtures might need replacement to comply with water conservation standards. Agents are typically aware of such requirements in their immediate localities and can usually advise clients accordingly.

2. *What repairs (if any) are specified in the purchase contract? In some contracts, special provisions are made for repairing particular problems; in those cases, sellers are required to address specific issues revealed by the inspector. Other contracts have no such provisions.*

3. *How motivated and negotiable is the seller? Market conditions and personal circumstances can make a big difference when determining requests and demands to present to a seller. In a "hot" real estate market, an as-is approach might be the best way to secure the deal. When the economy is slow, a seller might be willing to jump through hoops to complete the sale. Personal circumstances affecting a seller's negotiability might include a court-ordered sale, a divorce sale, an out-of-state residency, impending foreclosure, and the like. In those cases, sellers might be willing to make sacrifices, or they might be unable to do so.*

4. *How capable a negotiator is your agent? Brokers and agents come from divergent professional backgrounds, with different blends of strengths, abilities, and experience. Some may be great administrators, organizers, or motivators, but not everyone is a gifted negotiator. When it comes to haggling, your agent is your gladiator. Hopefully, that person will be equipped to effectively present your position.*

5. *Are you willing to walk away from the deal if you don't get what you want? Masters of negotiation say that the strongest negotiating position is the willingness to forego the entire deal if you don't get what you want. For many people, emotional attachment to the purchase, whether a home, a car, or a pair of shoes, negates this essential advantage. This does not mean that one should be so obstinate as to demand every preference with an "or else" approach. But where critical issues are at stake, emotional detachment is a valuable tool when discussing the terms of a sale.*

Finally, don't forget that a home inspection report is not a repair list for the seller. It is an information list for you, the buyer, to help you know what you are buying and to help you decide whether to proceed with the deal.

———————

These standards should be applied when reviewing the inspection report, as a means of separating repairs to be requested from conditions to be accepted. At this point, the buyers and their agent typically formulate a letter of request for the sellers. A wise approach for structuring this letter is to state that some defects will be accepted in as-is condition. Listing the items to be accepted is a good strategy for negotiation because enumerating the accepted defects demonstrates a willingness to be reasonable rather than demanding. The letter should then list the items for which repairs are requested, beginning with conditions required by law or by contract and concluding with the items that are subject to the sellers' approval. When submitting this letter to the sellers, it should include a copy of the home inspection report if the seller has not already received a copy.

ASK THE INSPECTOR

Buyer Questions Special Use Alterations

Dear Barry,

I am purchasing a home from someone who uses a wheelchair. Therefore, the house has some unusual alterations. Both entryways have ramps rather than stairs; the electrical switches are lower than usual; and special hardware has been installed in the bathroom. Are these considered defects and is the seller obligated to change these conditions?

Ruth

Dear Ruth,

When a property is altered for the convenience of a disabled person, these changes do not constitute defects, even though they could affect standard use by persons not in a wheelchair. In that light, disclosure of such conditions would be advisable for the seller, but restoration of the building to its original condition is not required. Nevertheless, all conditions are negotiable in the course of a real estate purchase. Therefore, changes to the property are always open for discussion between buyers and sellers.

THE RESPONSE OF SELLERS

Seller responses to repair requests vary widely according to circumstances and personalities, and buyers should not automatically expect *carte blanche* acceptance of their wish list. Most sellers will agree to fix portions of the buyers' listed concerns, a few will refuse to fix anything, and a small, but delightful, group of others will agree to fix everything.

The following are the three most common reasons for seller refusals:

1. The majority of sellers seek to obtain maximum financial advantage when selling a home. Thus their willingness to address needed repairs will be counterbalanced by monetary concerns. Just as buyers want to acquire property for the least amount possible, sellers want to relinquish ownership for the most they can reasonably get. This is business as usual—an expression of common human avarice.

2. Some sellers, although willing to make repairs, are financially unable to do so. Examples include sales resulting from foreclosure, bankruptcy, divorce, or court order.

3. The most difficult group, those who precipitate the most canceled sales, are sellers who are unwilling to make repairs for strictly personal and emotional reasons. Examples include those who believe they sold the property for less than it was worth. The most intractable holdouts, however, are sellers who built or remodeled their homes or who made the daily practice of impeccable maintenance an extension of their essential beings. These folks can become seriously irate at the mere mention of defects pertaining to their exalted workmanship.

ASK THE INSPECTOR

Negotiation Is Not Always Negotiable

Dear Barry,

   As a first-time homebuyer, I want to avoid costly mistakes. I've made an offer on a home, have signed a purchase contract, but am having trouble with the seller. He recently remodeled the house, but my home inspector found many problems with the work, as well as defects with the furnace and electrical wiring. According to the *agent, the seller is out of the country, with no phone access, yet he is somehow able to communicate by e-mail and has left word that he disagrees with all of the inspector's findings. He insists that all work was done properly and there are no problems with the building. How can I work out these differences if the seller won't communicate openly?*

Debra

Dear Debra,

Not all differences can be worked out. Successful negotiations, in any transaction, require that all parties act in good faith. If you find yourself stonewalled by a seller whose motives are suspect, you'd be wise to regard the impasse as fair warning—a red flag of impending consequence. As a general rule in real estate, another good deal is always around the corner.

You hired a professional home inspector to be your advocate, to provide you with unbiased information about the property in question, and to protect you from costly mistakes and needless misgivings. Now, the facts are in writing, the seller disagrees yet remains unavailable for discussion.

Many buyers have ignored telltale signs such as these, and many have suffered bitter regrets when the latent consequences became financially apparent. Reality can be very painful after the sale is completed. It's easier to leave the table with your money still in hand than to recoup your losses when the dealing is done. If the seller won't play with a full deck, there are other games in town.

Look out for number one: if you don't, who will?

When sellers flatly refuse to make specified repairs, buyers are faced with a critical choice: whether to cancel the transaction or accept the unrepaired defects as they are. Decisions of this kind hinge upon many factors: individual temperaments, personal circumstances, various contingencies of the sale, but, mainly, the financial implications of the problems needing repair.

When negotiations become deadlocked, a useful way of leveraging the conversation is to obtain repair bids from licensed contractors. Genuine numbers, particularly those that begin with dollar signs, add a dimension of reality to any discussion. Take the case of a foundation with large cracks and a seller who refuses to pay for structural upgrades. Negotiations have come to a standstill. But then the buyer decides to have a structural engineer or general contractor estimate the cost of repair for the foundation problem. Suddenly, the issue boils down to basic arithmetic. The buyer simply adds the appraised value of the property to the estimated repair costs. If the total does not exceed the sales price, then the purchase may still be acceptable. If the total does exceed the sales price, the seller's negotiating position is weakened. Another variation of this approach is to provide copies of the home inspection report and the contractor's repair bid to the real estate appraiser—the person who determines the official value of the property. This could prompt the appraiser to adjust the appraisal, thereby inducing the seller to adjust the sales price accordingly.

Possible scenarios involving deadlocked negotiations are endless and would constitute ample basis for a complete book on post-inspection negotiations.

DEALING WITH REPAIRS

In the majority of residential sales, repairs are performed as a result of the home inspection. This fact affects real estate sales procedures by making the complicated repair phase an expected element of the routine. The demanding process of arranging and orchestrating repairs can be complicated and time consuming and has become the *de facto* responsibility of agents for the buyers and sellers. Contractors and handymen must be contacted and scheduled in a time frame that coincides with the specified closing date for the sale. Scheduling must be coordinated with the daily routines of sellers, and all parties must agree that completed repairs were performed in an acceptable manner.

This last item—completeness and correctness of the work performed—raises an issue that is typically overlooked. In most cases, the home inspector is not asked to inspect the repair work that was done in connection with the inspection report. Instead, it is taken for granted that all items on the repair list were completed and that all such repairs were performed in a workmanlike manner, without errors or shortcuts. In a small minority of these transactions, the

Condition of shakes warrants reroofing, not partial repair.

home inspector is asked to evaluate and approve the repairs prior to closing the sale. The alarming reality here is that, when reinspected, these repairs are almost always found to be incomplete or incorrect in some respects. Because most transactions do not involve reinspection of repairs, one can only wonder which defects are presumed to be fully and properly repaired when, in fact, they are not. The obvious point here is that repairs should be subject to reinspection. The immediate consequence of such a practice would most likely be angry and embarrassed contractors and tradespeople, not to mention delayed closings of transactions. If reinspection were to become a common practice, the long-term consequence would be enhanced attention to quality workmanship in the performance of such repairs. If the people who perform these repairs were to anticipate an inspection, the quality of workmanship, in all likelihood, would noticeably improve. Until then, an alternate and advantageous approach for buyers would be to request a cash credit from the sellers, providing the buyers with funds to make repairs after purchasing the property.

ASK THE INSPECTOR

Agent Concerned about Foundation Repairs

Dear Barry,

As a Realtor, part of my job is to orchestrate the hiring and scheduling of contractors after my buyers have home inspections. In one case, the inspector disclosed a foundation problem, and I arranged for a general contractor to make repairs. But one year later, an engineer said the work was inadequate. I thought that I was doing the right thing, but now it seems that wasn't enough. What should I have done to prevent this situation?

George

Dear George,

Competent general contractors are qualified to perform foundation repairs, but evaluations of foundation problems should be done by licensed structural engineers before repair work is commenced. An engineer is the diagnostician best qualified to determine the causes of foundation failures and propose the necessary remedial prescriptions. When the contractor's work is directed by the engineer, the likelihood of solving the problem permanently is significantly increased. When faced with a foundation problem, the most prudent approach is to have it reviewed first by a licensed engineer.

CHAPTER NINE

Problems After
the Sale

Cleaning up the spilt milk.

DEFINING THE ISSUES

When faulty conditions are discovered after a property sale, costly and unpleasant messes can result. Sad examples could fill volumes. The complexities of this subject are too numerous for an in-depth analysis in this book, and therefore are addressed here in the context of broad general principles and recommended practices. The four major facets of this expansive topic are as follows:

1. *Appropriate versus inappropriate complaints:* Not all disclosure complaints are appropriate. There are undisclosed problems for which claims against sellers, agents, and home inspectors are reasonable and justified. In contrast, there are problems for which confrontation and complaints are totally out of place and unsuited to the circumstances.

2. *Known versus unknown defects:* Some defects are clearly known by the parties in the transaction and therefore require disclosure. In contrast, other defects are not disclosed because, for one reason or another, they are honestly unknown to anyone.

3. *Deliberate versus inadvertent nondisclosure:* Sometimes, undisclosed problems are known but deliberately concealed by some of the parties to the transaction. This is deliberate nondisclosure, a

case of bad intent. At other times, problems are innocently over-looked because someone failed to notice them or simply forgot to mention them at the time of sale. This is inadvertent nondis-closure, a case of bad luck.

4. *Acceptance and avoidance of disclosure responsibility:* When undis-closed problems are discovered after the sale and receive mean-ingful responses from sellers, agents, and home inspectors, we call this acceptance of disclosure liability. In contrast, when undisclosed problems are revealed after the sale and are unfairly sidestepped or ignored by some or all of the responsi-ble parties, we call this avoidance of disclosure liability.

ASK THE INSPECTOR

Finding Fault for Hidden Damage

Dear Barry,

Three years after buying my home, a heavy rainstorm caused flooding in the basement. The wall paneling had to be removed and revealed major foundation damage. This problem was not disclosed by the sellers, and my home inspector didn't find it because of the paneling. An engineer determined that the problem was due to an improperly installed drainage system. The contractor who installed the french drain agreed to pay $5,000, but the total repair costs are estimated at $20,000. Are the sellers of the home liable for the additional costs?

Robert

Dear Robert,

The basement foundation damage was apparently not visible to the sellers of your home. Likewise, the flooding problem may have been unknown to them, because it did not occur on an annual basis. Therefore, the sellers' position of deniability seems plausible and may preclude them from liability under the law. For confirmation, you should consult an attorney, but be cautious when soliciting legal advice in matters of this kind.

A common practice when lawyers are added to the mix is to coerce payments from perceived opponents regardless of the merits of the case. A well-worded letter on legal letterhead can be very intimidating, and people can be forced to make unfair settlements just to avoid the cost and stress of litigation.

The sellers, in your case, are in a position that could befall anyone. We market a home in good faith, and then three years later, a concealed problem rears its tentacles. Sometimes bad things happen in a transaction without any particular party being at fault.

Another avenue worth investigation is your homeowners insurance. Although such policies do not include drainage problems, they may cover structural damage that results from faulty drainage. Give your agent a call; you may just get lucky.

The interplay of these variables gives rise to countless unfortunate situations, expanding the files of real estate offices, the schedules of mediators and arbitrators, and the dockets of every municipal court in the land. Regardless of the causes or circumstances, delayed discoveries are the scourge of real estate transactions. They cause lost sleep, heightened tempers, and lucrative incomes for attorneys. In short, they are a leading source of legal and emotional trouble.

The best time to discover, negotiate, and resolve property defects is during the purchase process, when compromises can be made, modified, or canceled without financial consequence. After the close, the climate for discussion is less tolerant, less flexible, and sometimes rudely and expensively uncomfortable.

The surest protection against post-sale conflict is total disclosure, the focal point being a detailed home inspection prior to closing. Yet even with the best intentions of all parties to fully disclose, and with the utmost efforts of qualified home inspectors to discover defects, issues still emerge after sales are completed. In too many cases, the result is needless conflict. How to address these quagmires is the purpose of this chapter.

ASK THE INSPECTOR

Inspector May or May Not Have Made Error

Dear Barry,

We've got a gas pipe problem that our home inspector missed. Our plumber noticed a pipe running across our roof and down the living room wall to the fireplace and said it might violate code. If this gas line is illegal, shouldn't my home inspector have reported it? If so, is he liable to have it removed?

Michael

Dear Michael,

Your question does not indicate which code, if any, has been violated. The plumbing code specifies which pipe materials are safe and legal for conducting gas, minimum pipe sizes for particular applications, and locations that comply with safety requirements. Problems of this kind are typically reported by home inspectors. Lack of disclosure by your inspector indicates one of two things: either the gas line is properly installed or your inspector failed to notice an apparent defect. To determine which is the case, ask the plumber to explain the nature of the violation and to show you the requirement as stated in the code book. Once you have this information, call the home inspector for a reinspection of the gas line. If the inspection company is at fault, perhaps it will assist in correcting the problem.

APPROPRIATE VERSUS INAPPROPRIATE COMPLAINTS

Unwanted surprises are often found when buyers take possession of a home. These can range in severity from the least to the worst; from the modest to the grotesque; from minor cosmetic flaws (such as weathered paint or a scratched door) to common functional problems (such as a failed garbage disposal or an unopenable window), to significant safety hazards (such as a cracked gas furnace or bootlegged electrical wiring), or to major structural problems (such as a failed foundation or severe dry rot in the framing). A balanced understanding of these conditions is vital when you've just assumed ownership. The following guidelines will establish a reasonable perspective and can assist in avoiding regrettable decisions.

Minor Defects

In the emotional aftermath of a sale, the relevance of undisclosed problems can magnify and inflate in the minds of buyers, with large sums of repair moneys being demanded from sellers, agents, and home inspectors. Such demands are sometimes appropriate; sometimes not.

When minor defects are disclosed prior to sale, buyers typically regard them as background information not warranting immediate repair. For example, most buyers would not insist that sellers tighten loose faucet handles or clean the baked-on residue in the oven. Yet when these same problems are discovered after the close, some buyers can lose their smiles and become surprisingly confrontational. Minor conditions, such as doors that rub, window screens with feline claw marks, or chipped tiles around a sink—conditions that might have been taken in stride if disclosed prior to sale—may suddenly give rise to declarations of war when revealed later. Problems of small import may escalate to serious levels, not on their merits, but simply because no one made disclosure when the deal was in progress. The severity of the defect is no longer the issue: Now, by golly, it's the principle of the thing.

Advice to buyers. Recognize minor defects for what they are: the common lot of all homes, not a valid basis for putting on one's battle armor. Furthermore, don't pursue minor issues as a matter of principle; it's just not worth the aggravation. Instead, allow yourself the freedom to enjoy your new home. Yes, you're right, some of these problems should have been disclosed by the seller or listed in the home inspection report, but common sense should not be abandoned. If these defects had been disclosed during the transaction, repairs would probably not have been requested as a condition of the sale. Therefore, nondisclosure should be regarded as a minor oversight, not worthy of follow-up interactions with sellers, agents, or home inspectors.

ASK THE INSPECTOR

Buyers Find Defects Not Disclosed by Inspector

Dear Barry,

Since purchasing our home, we've found several items that were overlooked by our home inspector. We relied on his report and now are wondering what to do.

Carey

Dear Carey,

Give your inspector a call. Most home inspectors—the good ones, that is— expect buyers to let them know when problems materialize after the sale. Many inspectors encourage clients to call if and when concerns develop. Inspectors refer to these as "callbacks" and regard them as an inescapable aspect of doing business.

If an undisclosed building defect was visually discernible during the inspection, a competent inspector will arrange to have it corrected or to refund money as specified in the inspection agreement. If a problem was concealed at the time of the inspection or was specifically listed in the report as being outside the scope of the inspection, that condition would not be the inspector's responsibility.

Advice to others. One way to raise the ire of a dissatisfied buyer is to turn a cold shoulder to a complaint, even when the subject of the complaint is minor. The best way to lay a minor problem to rest is to demonstrate interest and concern. For sellers, this can allay needless appointments with the presiding judge of the local small claims court. For agents, it can reinforce good relations with former clients and add voices of support to a good reputation. For home inspectors, it can do all of the above and, at the same time, encourage recommendations for future business.

When buyers raise issues of complaint, these are the five steps to follow:

1. Contact the buyers immediately.

2. Make an appointment to visit the buyers at the property.

3. Be reasonable in your approach and hope that the buyers do the same.

4. Consider whether the buyers' claims are valid.

5. If valid, negotiate as fair a resolution as possible.

ASK THE INSPECTOR

Inspector Missed Illegal Plumbing Connection

Dear Barry,

When we bought our home, our inspector said nothing about the discharge pipe from the water softener. But this week our plumber said that it is illegally connected to a sewer line. It hasn't given us any trouble, but the plumber says it could contaminate our drinking water. How could our inspector have missed this?

Tom

Dear Tom,

Connecting a water softener discharge pipe to a sewer drain is a definite code violation and, unfortunately, one that occurs in many homes. An elemental aspect of the plumbing code is the protection of water supply systems from sources of contamination. Essential to this objective is a general prohibition against direct hookups between water supply lines and sewer piping. Wherever such connections exist, there is the possibility of back-siphonage, with the potential for infecting the domestic drinking water.

In the event of a sewage backup, raw effluent could be forced through the discharge pipe and into the water softener. From there, bacteria and protozoa could thoroughly contaminate your water supply. With a standpipe, instead of a direct pipe connection, a sewage backup would cause spillage only without affecting your drinking water.

This should be corrected as soon as possible and should be called to the attention of your home inspector.

KNOWN VERSUS UNKNOWN DEFECTS

Undisclosed defects can arise for various good, bad, or indifferent reasons. On the innocent side, they may simply have been concealed from view, unknowable to the most well-intentioned sellers, agents, and inspectors. They could have been hidden beneath siding, plaster, wallboard, storage, furnishings, landscaping, or any number of other objects. Fixtures and appliances may have been in good working order at the time of sale, but latent internal defects might have caused them to fail shortly after the close. A nonpermitted addition may have been built by a previous owner, unbeknownst to the current seller. The sellers may have inherited the property and have been completely unfamiliar with its best and worst characteristics. The shortcomings of contractors and technicians who worked on the property may not have been realized by the sellers, and resultant flaws may not have been apparent on the surface. The scenarios are endless.

Countless lawsuits are born in the wake of real estate sales, when unknown defects suddenly come to light. Many such claims are justified and are addressed in a later section of this chapter. Many others, however, are filed against persons who performed in good faith yet were blamed for defects that were beyond the pale of reasonable discovery. When confronted with undisclosed defects, buyers should consider whether those conditions were known or likely to have been known by the participants in the transaction.

The dockets of courtrooms are littered with frivolous cases involving faulty plumbing or electrical conditions that were concealed within walls until a remodeling project brought them to light, or a furnace with an internal crack that could not have been discovered without dismantling the fixture. When such discoveries occur, buyers may feel unfairly saddled with the unexpected repair costs. This is a natural reaction; but to conclude that the sellers, agents, and inspectors are to blame may be equally unfair. Unfortunate circumstances are not always someone's fault. Sometimes bad things just happen. There are instances when blame can be fairly assigned and times when the shoe of guilt just doesn't fit. The fair response to an unfair outcome is not further unfairness.

ASK THE INSPECTOR

Newly Purchased Home Plagued by Water Leaks

Dear Barry,

Our home inspector didn't let us know about the excess water pressure in our plumbing. After we moved in, the dishwasher hose ruptured, spewing water over the hardwood floor and carpet. Our plumber said the pressure is 160 pounds. We think the seller and the home inspector should have disclosed this problem. Do we have any recourse?

Stan

Dear Stan,

This may be a case where no one is truly to blame. It is entirely possible that the seller was not aware of the problem, as high water pressure is not always apparent at plumbing fixtures. What's more, the pressure regulator could have failed after you purchased the property.

Home inspectors typically test water pressure as part of a plumbing evaluation. If your inspector measured the pressure, the reading at the time of the inspection should be indicated in the report. If not, you should give the inspector a call regarding this aspect of the inspection.

According to the plumbing code, residential water pressure should not exceed 80 psi (pounds per square inch). But excessive pressure is common in many areas and is usually known only to the plumbers who work in those neighborhoods. The high pressure in your home indicates that the water supply tank for the area is located at a high elevation in relation to your property. Water pressure is directly proportional to the vertical distance between the house and the supply tank. Therefore, in a hillside neighborhood, the farther down the hill a home is located, the higher its water pressure will be.

Surprisingly, most water companies take no steps to regulate residential water pressures or to inform property owners when pressures are excessive. Service meters are not equipped to maintain legal pressure limits, which leaves homeowners at the mercy of whatever pressures might happen to prevail.

Advice to buyers. A wise approach to known versus unknown defects is much the same as with minor defects in the previous section of this chapter. There are situations that warrant taking a stand, and there are times when it is best to stand down. Recognizing the essential difference is critical. Failure to correctly differentiate between valid and invalid claims can spawn needless legal collisions. To avoid unreasonable claims after purchasing a home, buyers should maintain realistic expectations about disclosure. Common sense and reasonableness should be exercised when blame is assigned for defects that may not have been apparent. This may not coincide with your attorney's advice. The choice, therefore, is to strike a balance between what is legal and what is right.

Advice to others. As with claims involving minor defects, sellers, agents, and home inspectors are strongly urged (spelled w-a-r-n-e-d) to take the concerns of buyers very seriously. The initial letter or phone call from a dissatisfied buyer is a critical fork in the road for your peace of mind and financial well-being. How you respond at that juncture can determine whether the avenue you take is labeled Litigation Highway or Resolution Street.

And remember the five essential steps for resolving complaints of nondisclosure:

1. Contact the buyers immediately.

2. Make an appointment to visit the buyers at the property.

3. Be reasonable in your approach and hope that the buyers do the same.

4. Consider whether the buyers' claims are valid.

5. Negotiate as fair a resolution as possible.

In this case, however, there is an additional sixth step:

6. If the buyers firmly insist that you pay for costly repairs when you are truly not liable, the time for legal counsel will have arrived.

ASK THE INSPECTOR

Our Home Inspector Was Wrong about Safety Glass

Dear Barry,

When we bought our house, the home inspector said the sliding glass door did not have safety glass. Last week we had our windows cleaned, and the window washer showed us the safety glass label at the lower corner of the door. Fortunately, we discovered this before wasting a lot of money on new glass. We were surprised that a 35-year-old home has safety glass and are wondering how this could have been missed by the inspector?

Leslie

Dear Leslie,

Sliding glass doors installed before the late 1960s seldom contain tempered glass. If the door in your home does have safety glass, it may be a replacement and not the original pane. If so, it is possible that the adjacent window panel is still the original plate glass, which might account for the home inspector's having disclosed the lack of safety glass.

To determine whether both panes are tempered, carefully check the corners of each for the safety glass emblem. If you find that either pane is not safety glass, replacement is advisable. A less costly alternative is to have a clear plastic film laminated onto the glass, but tempered glass provides better protection from personal injury.

DELIBERATE VERSUS INADVERTENT NONDISCLOSURE

Minor defects, as we have seen, are not worthy of conflict, and defects that are not apparent do not provide a fair basis for confrontation. The justifiable battleground for nondisclosure is where observable problems of a significant nature—conditions that must have been known—are discovered after the sale. Thus we embark upon the thorniest of disclosure topics: willful intent to withhold pertinent information about the property.

A primary difficulty regarding withheld disclosure is a legal one. You can prove that a defect exists, and you can prove that it was apparent and reasonably discoverable. What is not easy to prove is the intent of those persons being blamed for nondisclosure. Sometimes incriminating circumstances exist, and sometimes they don't. For example, let's take a main sewer line that becomes clogged two weeks after you buy your home. Your plumber determines that the entire line from the house to the street needs replacement for a total cost of $4,800. Your first reaction is to give the sellers the benefit of the doubt, to assume that they had no idea this problem existed. But then the neighbor tells you that a local plumber had to clear the line every few months. You contact that plumbing company and learn that the seller was advised to replace the line. This would constitute a clear case of failure to disclose a known defect.

Here's another example involving the same house: Six months after buying the property, the rainy season begins, and along with it the surprise roof leaks. Nothing was said about this during the purchase period, and you recall that the interior had just been repainted, thereby eliminating ceiling stains. You contact the seller, who insists that no previous leaking had occurred. It's his word against your unsubstantiated suspicions. But your purchase file contains the seller's receipt for the painting, so you decide to call the painter. He remembers having primed several ceiling stains, and these just happened to be in the same places where leaking recently occurred. Once again, you have a case of a seller concealing a known defect.

In this latter instance, the home inspector might also be culpable for not disclosing apparent roof defects. There are cases where roofs without apparent defects have been known to leak, but this is rare. Typically, leaky roofs have observable flaws that warrant attention by a roofing contractor and should be pointed out by a home inspector. Where ceiling stains have been concealed with paint, attic stains are likely to be apparent, and the locations of such stains often coincide with observable roof defects. If such defects were apparent at the time of the home inspection but were not specified in the report, then the inspector could be liable on the basis of having failed to report an observable defect that was within the scope of the inspection.

In either of these two cases, an agent could also bear responsibility for nondisclosure. For example, let's suppose that there had been a pending sale of the property three months before you decided to buy it. The buyer in that transaction may have canceled the purchase for any number of common reasons—finances, condition of the property, and so on. But let's say that the prospective buyer in that deal had hired a home inspector who disclosed roof defects, the potential for leakage, and evidence of past problems with the sewer line. Copies of that inspection report would have been given to the agent, fully disclosing those concerns; yet when you purchased the property, no mention was made of roof or sewer problems. In that case, the guns of deliberate nondisclosure would be squarely aimed at the agent.

ASK THE INSPECTOR

Our Inspector Missed Two Apparent Problems

Dear Barry,

We recently purchased a six-year-old home and hired a home inspector to check it out. Two weeks after moving in, we found two problems that he missed. There is a leak under the kitchen sink, and the stains indicate that the leaking is not new. Also, the bathroom wall seems to have moved slightly, causing the linoleum to buckle. What is your advice?

Sallie

Dear Sallie,

The basic scope of a home inspection is to discover visually discernible defects. A leaking drain, resultant water stains, a shifted wall, and apparent floor damage would seem to fit that definition. Most home inspection contracts limit the monetary extent of liability, but the conditions you've discovered may not involve major expense.

Your first course of action is to call these issues to the attention of the inspector and to request a reinspection of those areas. Reputable inspectors are willing to review conditions they may have missed. Give this a try and see what your inspector is willing to do.

For home inspectors, the ultimate dread is that phone call, letter, or summons arising from a defect that was not disclosed in the course of an inspection. A commonly heard allegation is that home inspectors deliberately withhold information in collusion with unscrupulous agents. Although such cases of conspiracy do exist, they are very rare. No home inspector could routinely ignore property defects without being overcome with claims and lawsuits for undisclosed problems. Allegations of agent-inspector collusion are inflated in the collective public mind by television journalists promoting sensationalism at the expense of balanced reporting. More commonly, home inspector errors and omissions occur because the inspector was unqualified, negligent, or just simply human. Regardless of the circumstances, inspectors bear varying degrees of liability for failure to disclose apparent defects. When surprises are discovered by buyers after the sale, home inspectors are viewed as professional experts in discovery and disclosure. They are held to higher standards of accountability than are sellers and agents and, therefore, can find themselves in very uncomfortable positions.

ASK THE INSPECTOR

Agents and Inspectors Accused of Collusion

Dear Barry,

How reliable are home inspections really? I've heard that home inspectors are all in league with Realtors—finding as few problems as possible to help close deals and secure future business. Let's see you defend that!

Arlen

Dear Arlen,

You don't waste time getting to the point, so I won't either. Notwithstanding the sensational exposés on television magazine shows, sordid relations between home inspectors and Realtors are not nearly as prevalent as you might believe.

Although instances of collusion between agents and inspectors have been known to occur, conspiracies of this kind are highly uncommon. In fact, many home inspectors have built solid reputations for thorough, detailed reporting, and there are many agents who routinely promote and demand full disclosure of property defects. They are the professionals whom we might call "advocates," because they truly represent the best interests of their clients. Sadly, there are also some misguided individuals whose tendency is to abbreviate the disclosure process and who regard the more thorough inspectors as "deal killers." We won't discuss appellations appropriate to those persons, but be thankful they are not the majority.

Home inspectors should be judged as individuals, not as a faceless group. Measure them instead by their overall knowledge, general experience, and reputations for personal integrity. Collusion with real estate professionals may exist, but such arrangements are rare. As in any profession, a few bad apples can give the whole barrel a foul odor.

Disclosure shortcomings by sellers, agents, or home inspectors are generally unintended, but cases of deliberate concealment are real and far more common than they should be. Thousands of actual and hypothetical examples could be cited. Sellers or agents may have withheld known information, fearing the loss of the sale; home inspectors may have overlooked apparent defects due to negligence, or an inspector may have pandered to an unprincipled agent to encourage future referrals. Examples are endless, giving rise to protracted conflicts, damaged reputations, and costly legal debacles.

Advice to buyers. When undisclosed problems are realized, steps can be taken against those who are liable; but some situations provide little opportunity for legal or financial remedy. Here are some examples: The sellers have moved out of state, making contact and legal processes difficult, if not impossible; the sellers have no financial assets, leaving you with no one against whom to file a claim; the sellers are ready, willing, and able to finance years of legal resistance, forcing you to pay large legal sums in pursuit of justice.

As for agent liability, there may have been no agent in the transaction, or if there was, the agent may have been totally unaware of problems that were concealed by the seller.

The home inspector, as is sometimes the case, may have been a part-timer with few financial assets and no errors and omissions insurance. In other words, the inspector may also have no assets worthy of pursuit.

In most instances, however, the following nine procedures should be followed immediately after discovery of undisclosed problems:

1. Contact the sellers, agents, and home inspector immediately, informing them of the problems you have discovered and requesting that they meet you at the property for an inspection and discussion of pertinent issues. Initial contact can be made by phone. If the response is unsatisfactory, certified letters may be necessary. Such letters usually elicit a response, as they are generally regarded as precursors to legal action.

2. Defects should not be altered or repaired in any way prior to review by all parties to the transaction. If repairs take place before everyone can view the disputed conditions, the nature of those conditions becomes a matter of your word against theirs.

3. When meeting at the property or elsewhere, be reasonable in your approach and hope that everyone else behaves likewise.

Proposing that other people take financial responsibility for property defects may not be well received. Few people simply say, "No problem. I'll call my contractor right away," or "Here, let me get my checkbook." One way or another, expect some haggling, with good or not-so-good results at the end of a short or long process.

4. Be willing to compromise. You may get lucky and receive what you want, but, then again, you may get only a partial solution, and although this may not be what you are entitled to, the difference may be less costly than the alternative legal battle. And as noted earlier, don't pursue a total solution as a matter of principle—that can cost you more in the long run than you're ever likely to gain.

5. If no one is willing to share in the cost of repairs, the time for legal representation may have arrived. Sometimes the implied seriousness of that step is sufficient to motivate a favorable response—attorney letters can be intimidating—but this could also be the first step in a costly and lengthy legal process.

6. If there is evidence of nondisclosure by a real estate professional, a complaint can be filed with the state agency that licenses agents and brokers.

7. If the home is brand-new and the developer refuses to make necessary repairs, it may be possible to file a complaint with the state agency that licenses contractors.

8. Whenever possible, try to settle disputes through mediation or arbitration. If successful, this can be much less costly and protracted than litigation.

9. If the dollar amount of repairs is not too large, it may be possible to file a suit in small claims court. That could provide you with a legal judgment in just a few weeks or months and at nominal expense.

ASK THE INSPECTOR

We Can't Find Our Light Switch

Dear Barry,

About a week after moving into my home, I went to turn on the patio light but could not find the switch. Turns out, there simply is no switch for that fixture. Shouldn't the home inspector have found this problem, and shouldn't the sellers have disclosed it? They were the original owners of the home and certainly should have known.

Rufus

Dear Rufus,

The sellers were probably aware of this problem and should have disclosed it, but it may have simply slipped their minds. This is the kind of defect that homeowners often grow accustomed to and fail to remember when asked to disclose problems. Nevertheless, they may be liable for nondisclosure.

Likewise, your home inspector could have found this defect. Most home inspectors check the majority of lights and switches but not necessarily every single one. In fact, many home inspection reports specify that only a random sampling of switches will be tested. Notwithstanding this disclaimer, most reputable home inspectors would be willing to pay for this type of correction for the purpose of maintaining good client relations and promoting a solid business reputation.

A positive approach would be to contact the sellers and the home inspector. A concerned inspector will gladly take a second look at this condition, and an ethical seller will recognize the need to make good on an undisclosed defect.

Advice to sellers. Those who withhold defect information when selling property have obvious ethical infirmities, and it is not the purpose of this book to educate them in that regard. It was the job of their parents to impart the essential differences between right and wrong, honest and dishonest, truthfulness and obfuscation. If such tutelage did not occur, then the threat of legal recourse for nondisclosure will hopefully induce proper behavior.

Failure to provide a buyer with full disclosure is an unethical form of gambling. When you bet and lose, it's time to pay the dealer. If, on the other hand, you simply forgot to list a particular defect in your disclosure statement, then you have committed an innocent human error. Unfortunately, innocent human errors can also be costly. The bottom line is to consider how you would view the situation if you were the buyer. When the buyer informs you of an undisclosed defect, respond as you would hope and expect if you were in that person's position.

ASK THE INSPECTOR

What to Do with the Old Inspection Report

Dear Barry,

What happens to a home inspection report when the deal is canceled? My home was recently being purchased, but the buyers backed out after the inspection. When the next buyers come along, do I have to disclose the findings of that inspection report, or is it up to them to provide their own inspection?

Marianne

Dear Marianne,

The next buyers of your home have the option to hire another home inspector, but this has no bearing on your obligation to disclose. When selling a home, owners must provide a list of all known defects. This means you must divulge every material fact you possess, regardless of where or when that information was obtained.

When your recent transaction was in progress, you had to disclose every pertinent fact you knew at that time. When you received the home inspection report, the level of your knowledge about the condition of your property was significantly increased. Whether that deal was completed is immaterial. You have now acquired new information about the physical state of your home. Withholding that information from subsequent buyers would be unethical and illegal and would subject you to significant liability exposure. Discovery of undisclosed defects after the sale would be incriminating if it were learned that the findings of a previous home inspection had been withheld.

Regardless of circumstances, the bottom line on seller disclosure is "disclose all that you know, without exception, without dilution, without compromise." In most states, that's the law. In every state, it's the smart thing, the safe thing, the right thing to do. When it comes to real estate disclosure, be proactive. Reveal everything. You'll sleep better after you sell and reduce the likelihood of days and dollars wasted in court.

Advice to agents. State disclosure laws are particularly strict for agents, generally requiring full disclosure of all conditions that would be of concern to a buyer. The legal and financial liability associated with undisclosed defects can be devastating for those in the real estate profession. Wise Realtors have learned this lesson well. They encourage total disclosure by sellers, they demand it of themselves, and they recommend the most thorough and experienced home inspectors. Furthermore, they regard with dismay those foolish agents who label the better inspectors as "deal killers" and who try to discourage their clients from using the most qualified inspectors available. Yet none of these good practices can guarantee protection against claims, they just improve the odds. Abundant complaints against honest, professional agents testify to this fact.

When claims occur, they must be addressed forthrightly, regardless of circumstances. Too many agents have been known to ignore such demands—when claims are frivolous, when the amounts of money being demanded are very large, or when ethical standards are deficient. In these cases, the advice just given for sellers applies as well to agents. Put yourself in the place of the buyer and respond as you would hope to be responded to if you were in that position.

Advice to home inspectors. As detailed in Chapter 7, home inspectors have varying degrees of liability according to the state laws where they do business. Many home inspection contracts contain provisions for limiting the monetary extent of liability, and the applicability of such limits can vary from one state to another. But these legal aspects are overshadowed, in some cases, by higher considerations.

How a home inspector responds when a claim arises is a personal business decision each inspector must make. Some inspectors will strongly disagree with the following advice, but here it is: Legal and contractual limits on liability should be used as protection against unfair claims only—against demands involving defects that were not discoverable or were outside the scope of the inspection. But where buyer demands involve negligent failure to disclose, home inspectors should adopt a more fair-minded perspective. This is where the five-step approach listed earlier comes into play. Again:

1. Contact the buyers immediately.

2. Make an appointment to visit the buyers at the property.

3. Be reasonable in your approach and hope that the buyers are too.

4. Consider whether the buyers' claims are valid.

5. Negotiate as fair a resolution as possible.

If needed repairs exceed the financial ability of the inspector, that's the purpose of insurance. Unfortunately, the practical application of errors and omissions insurance (E&O) has been to wait for a lawsuit to be filed and then defer the matter to the insurer. Another problem with E&O insurance is that many home inspectors do not carry it. Some states require inspectors to be insured, but others do not. Many inspectors avoid E&O for fear that the "deep pockets" provided by the insurance company will invite lawsuits. Litigation, as it is commonly practiced by today's legal profession, lends credibility to that concern.

Notwithstanding these many legal complications, home inspectors are advised to do what is practical, fair, and honest as the specifics of each situation indicate. Home inspectors are in the business of consumer advocacy and should approach their customer relationships in that way, responding affirmatively to reasonable claims and dealing forthrightly with those that are not so reasonable.

ASK THE INSPECTOR

Seller Unsure about Disclosing a Repaired Problem

Dear Barry,

The people who are buying my house hired a home inspector. The inspector found the upstairs toilet to be loose and recommended tightening the floor bolts. A few days later, water began dripping from the downstairs ceiling, directly below the toilet. I had the leak corrected and repaired the water damage at the ceiling. The buyers don't know that the leak occurred, and I'm wondering: Now that it's been repaired, does it need to be disclosed?

Ronda

Dear Ronda,

The best answer to any disclosure question is to disclose all that you know or that could possibly be of concern to a buyer. When in doubt, disclose. If a problem has been thoroughly repaired, there is no reason to withhold the information. In fact, if the problem were to reoccur and the buyers were to learn that it was not the first leak at that location, they might assume that you had deliberately withheld knowledge of an ongoing problem.

The best and safest approach is to air the issue now. Most buyers would appreciate the fact that you are being so thorough in your disclosures, that you would mention conditions that are no longer problems. This approach can help to assure buyers that they are dealing with someone who is honest and who is trying to do the right thing.

ACCEPTANCE AND AVOIDANCE OF DISCLOSURE RESPONSIBILITY

As stated at the outset of this chapter, there are instances where undisclosed property defects are discovered after the sale and receive substantial responses from sellers, agents, and home inspectors. As also stated, there are undisclosed problems that, when revealed after the sale, are unfairly sidestepped or ignored. Most of what can be said about this has been covered in the previous sections of this chapter. To recap, here are the main points:

- Sellers and agents are required in most states to provide full disclosure of all known defects. Failure to comply is a violation of the law in those states. Failure to disclose in the absence of such laws is a violation of common ethical decency.

- Home inspectors are professionally accountable for disclosure of defects that are visually discernible and within the defined scope of the inspection. Failure to disclose such conditions constitutes negligence.

- Sellers, agents, and home inspectors should respond to a buyer's repair demands in a manner that is consistent with the validity of the claim. A personal response and sincere demonstration of concern should be made in the case of each claim.

- Every reasonable effort should be made to settle disputes in ways that are fair, equitable, and appropriate to the situation. "Stonewalling" is strongly discouraged. It's a risky form of gambling, based upon the hope that a problem ignored is a problem solved. If this "head-in-the-sand" approach doesn't work, the cost could be years of litigation.

- Responses should be made with a balanced consideration of the buyers' perspective. To the new owners of a home, the transaction of the sale is the beginning, not the end, of the purchase process. For them, the sale is an ongoing reality. To sellers, agents, and home inspectors, the deal, after the close, is finalized history. For them, problems discovered in the aftermath of the sale can feel like waking up to a bad dream. Escaping from this dream to a more pleasant reality can depend upon the responses offered to the buyers. A hasty, flippant response can trap everyone in the same scary and protracted nightmare.

ASK THE INSPECTOR

Verbal Disclosures versus Written Ones

Dear Barry,

While remodeling our new home, our contractor discovered that the house once had a fire. When I called my agent about this, he said that old fire damage had been fully disclosed to me during the transaction. None of the paperwork mentions anything about a fire, but the agent, the seller, and the home inspector all insist that I was informed verbally of this condition. What good are written disclosures if they can be overruled by what was supposedly said?

Bridgette

Dear Bridgette,

Written disclosure is the centerpiece of every residential real estate transaction. No fact is more indelibly etched into the minds and hearts of home inspectors and Realtors. Oral disclosure is vapor on a windy day. Who can say, on the morrow, whether it appeared this way or that? Written disclosure, on the other hand, is the indisputable meat and potatoes of purchase information. If verbal claims were preeminent over written ones, disputes and suits would become the aftermath of far more home sales than is presently the case.

For home inspectors, the written report is the formal, final, and factual declaration of what was discovered, in total, about the property. This is the standard of the home inspection industry. What is written overshadows what anyone might claim to have said.

When a home inspector discovers evidence of a past fire, disclosure to the buyer is imperative, even if there is no serious damage to the structure. If the damage is superficial, then the report should make a statement such as this: "Evidence of past fire was noted in the attic. No significant damage was observed. Consult local fire department for a copy of the fire report." On the other hand, if serious fire damage is observed, the inspector might say: "Evidence of fire damage was noted in the attic. Refer to a licensed general contractor for replacement or repair of damaged framing, and consult fire department for a copy of the fire report." But to say nothing in the report, while mentioning the condition only by way of oral conversation, would constitute negligent performance on the part of a professional home inspector.

Likewise, within the real estate profession, there is total emphasis on the need for pinpoint disclosure throughout every transaction. No aspect of the real estate business has been so thoroughly driven into the minds of Realtors during the past 10 to 15 years. As part of every sale, an agent conducts what is known as a "due diligence" inspection and submits a written form, disclosing all conditions that were observed or otherwise discovered. And again, these disclosures are not to be merely spoken. They must be inscribed on paper and signed.

Furthermore, in most states agents must counsel their sellers in the filing of a complete disclosure statement in which a seller lists every known condition that could possibly affect a buyer's decision to complete the transaction.

With all three parties in your transaction having failed to provide written disclosure of a significant condition, alleged oral disclosures would certainly appear to be suspect. Something is not right with this picture.

———————————

CHAPTER TEN

Homebuyer's Inspection Checklist

Don't try to do this at home.

Homebuyers often request a comprehensive prepurchase checklist to use before hiring a home inspector, a list that enables the average buyer to perform preliminary property inspection and pinpoint major defects and problems. Such lists have been offered by well-intentioned home inspectors and other consumer advocates, but they are plagued with two inherent problems:

1. Checklists do not qualify the average homebuyer to recognize or evaluate the countless symptoms of significant property defects.

2. All checklists are abridged; none contain all of the potential problems likely to be found by a qualified home inspector.

In short, neither the checklist nor the average homebuyer is equal to the task of reliable defect discovery.

The purpose of the following list, therefore, is *not* to equip a homebuyer to perform a reliable home inspection. Rather, it is to provide a basic understanding, presented in layman's terms, of the general content of a detailed home inspection report. This checklist should help buyers to understand the information presented by their inspector; provide a framework of expectations prior to the inspection; and enable buyers to gauge the thoroughness of the home inspection itself.

Buyers often view the home inspection process as a veiled mystery, presumed to exceed the comprehension of all but the duly initiated and divinely anointed. Inspections are particularly mysterious to buyers who have no construction-related experience; to whom the depths of plumbing and electrical defects appear as impenetrable as the esoteric aspects of quantum physics. There are, of course, building technicalities that require specialized knowledge and experience and that call for years of professional exposure. This, however, does not prevent persons without such knowledge from comprehending the basic findings of a home inspection.

The following, therefore, is a list of the most common conditions likely to be discovered by your home inspector, with explanatory comments for each item.

FOUNDATION CHECKLIST

Many homebuyers see foundational stability as the primary focus and concern of a home inspection. In the real world of home inspections, foundation problems are among the least common of all property defects. Nevertheless, foundation evaluation is a vital consideration when inspecting a home, because defects in this area can overshadow the importance of all other property issues. In short, foundation problems are important albeit rare. With this understanding, the following conditions are the main elements of a foundation inspection:

1. ☐ **Common cracks.** Hairline stress cracks are typically found at portions of most foundations. Concrete and masonry are relatively inflexible materials, and because the earth is not rigidly static, normal ground movement usually causes minor cracks. Homebuyers should not be concerned about cracks of this kind.

Common hairline foundation cracks, such as this one, do not warrant concern.

Major foundation crack warrants evaluation by a licensed structural engineer.

2. ☐ **Large or displaced cracks.** When cracks exceed ⅛ inch in width or when the two sides of a crack are misaligned due to differential movement, further evaluation by a licensed structural engineer is usually warranted.

ASK THE INSPECTOR

Engineer Slighted by Inspector's Opinion

Dear Barry,

In a previous column, you downplayed the advantages of structural engineers who perform home inspections. You stated that "to limit the scope of a home inspection to purely structural considerations drastically reduces the accepted standards of practice for a physical inspection." Shouldn't you clarify that structural problems are also of concern and that an engineer's inspection may also be needed?

Peter, Structural Engineer

Dear Peter,

By all means, structural defects in a home are of particular concern to home inspectors, and evaluations by licensed engineers are warranted when such conditions are discovered. But problems of this nature are not the only important concerns when inspecting a home, nor do they represent the most commonly found major defects. My intention, therefore, is not to minimize the qualifications and relevance of structural engineers, but to stress that far more is at stake in the performance of a home inspection and that engineering credentials by themselves are not wholly sufficient in meeting the demands of a home inspection.

Some homebuyers assume that structural analysis is the primary focus of a home inspection. They hire an inspector purely for assurance of the structural integrity of a home. In the real world of property defects, structural problems occur in a small minority of cases. On the other hand, problems involving function and safety can be found to greater or lesser degrees in all homes. Understanding this basic premise provides homebuyers with a broader view of the scope and purpose of a home inspection.

3. ☐ **Deterioration of foundations.** Concrete and masonry foundations can become
soft and crumbly, especially in older homes.
This can be due to substandard composition
of the materials or years of exposure to excessive ground water. Conditions of this kind
warrant evaluation by a licensed structural
engineer.

Concrete pier is deteriorated and prone to crumbling. Replacement is warranted.

4. ☐ **Dimensions of foundations.** Aboveground portions of foundations should be
checked to determine that size and layout
are in accordance with accepted building standards. Buried portions of foundations are also subject to question but are not within the scope of a home
inspection, as excavation would be necessary to enable evaluation.

5. ☐ **Anchor bolts or straps.** Bolting or strapping of the framing to the foundation has
been required since the mid-1930s. Anchor
bolts and straps should be checked for condition and proper placement. When homes are
built on a concrete slab foundation, it is usually not possible to inspect this hardware except at open-framed walls in garages.

Some loose nut forgot to fasten the hardware.

6. ☐ **Seismic reinforcement.** Structural standards for homes are increased from time to
time, especially as they relate to earthquake resistance. Older homes are typically not in compliance with current standards. Although upgrades are not
required in most areas, home inspectors routinely point out when buildings
could benefit from added support.

7. ☐ **Posts and piers.** Many homes with concrete foundations at their perim-
eters have posts and piers to support the interior portions of the structure.
Common defects with posts and piers include substandard materials, faulty
placement, lack of adequate attachment, earth-to-wood contact, rotted
wood, deteriorated concrete, leaning, settlement, and so on.

8. ☐ **Substandard repairs.** Substandard foundation repairs indicate that
structural problems have been addressed by unqualified persons, without the
benefit of review by a structural expert. Examples include added concrete
poured against foundations, added hardware at concrete cracks, mortar

packed into settlement gaps, stacked bricks or wood blocks in lieu of piers, added posts in contact with soil, wood shims at piers and sill plates, and so on.

Faulty framing conditions below this home include one leaning post, one displaced post, and earth-to-wood contact.

Foundations repair, courtesy of Harry Homeowner.

ASK THE INSPECTOR

Problem with Subfloor Vapor Barrier

Dear Barry,

The insulation under my home was installed upside down, that is, with the vapor barrier facing the ground rather than against the subfloor. Is this a serious problem? Also, does the material need to be replaced, or can it simply be reversed and reattached?

Bonnie

Dear Bonnie,

Installing subfloor insulation with the vapor barrier on the downward side can cause moisture condensation on the framing and subfloor. Possible consequences include dryrot and mold infestation. Hopefully, this has not occurred beneath your home, but to make sure that no such problems have developed, the insulation should be removed to enable inspection of the wood framing and subfloor surfaces. This evaluation should be done by a licensed pest control operator (commonly known as a termite inspector).

If removal of the insulation is done carefully, you should be able to reuse the material by simply turning it over and resecuring it to the framing. If you do the work yourself, be sure to wear a high-quality respirator.

9. ☐ **Sloped floors.** Floors that are out of level often indicate building settlement. With modern homes, which are subject to contemporary building standards, this would arouse concern in the course of an inspection. In older homes, which were built prior to the advent of current structural standards, uneven floors could indicate a major problem or merely normal settlement consistent with age. Home inspectors, in these cases, must determine whether an engineering evaluation is warranted.

10. ☐ **Large cracks in walls.** Common cracks are to be expected at interior and exterior walls of most homes. Larger cracks, however, may indicate more than the usual movement of the structure and may warrant evaluation by a licensed structural engineer.

Uneven slab floor could be due to settlement, lifting, faulty installation of concrete, or a substandard building addition.

Common crack in old plaster wall; typical of normal building stresses.

11. ☐ **Misaligned doors and windows.** Rubbing or binding at doors and windows could be due to problems with those specific fixtures or could indicate settlement of the building. Accompanying symptoms, such as cracks or sloping, usually help in making this type of evaluation.

12. ☐ **Inadequate ground clearance.** Substandard clearance beneath a building prevents total inspection of the structure and indicates that the building was constructed without attention to applicable building standards. Inadequate clearance can also prevent an adequate inspection and complicate the performance of needed repair work.

Substandard ground clearance below building.

GRADING AND DRAINAGE CHECKLIST

Faulty site grading and ground drainage problems are responsible for some of the most costly forms of property damage. Groundwater can undermine foundations, rot subfloor framing, lift a concrete slab floor, promote mold infestation, flood basements, attract termites, and so on. The symptoms of faulty drainage, especially during the dry season, can be nearly unobservable, except to those with professional expertise in identifying such conditions. With this basic understanding, pertinent conditions when inspecting a home are as follows:

1. □ **Ground sloped toward building.**
Ground surfaces that slope toward a building can cause major moisture problems, including flooding of basements and crawlspaces and various damages associated with flooding. Surface drainage is among the most vital conditions to be considered when inspecting a property.

Front yard is sloped to drain toward building.

2. □ **Signs of ponding near building.** Faulty grade conditions can cause water to pool near a building, a condition known as ponding. In dry weather, low or depressed areas should be noted as potential problems in this regard.

3. □ **Flower beds trapping water at foundation.** Garden areas around a building are often lower than the surrounding grade, promoting ponding during wet weather and when irrigation systems are operated.

Severe ponding occurs at front porch during rainy weather.

Further clogging of yard drain will cause ponding in garden area and possible water intrusion into building.

4. □ **Evidence of past flooding below building.** Signs of past flooding below a building include ground surfaces that have the look of a dry lake bed, high-water lines on the foundations, erosion due to surface water flow, and

dried mud on materials above grade level. Further review by a geotechnical engineer is usually warranted.

5. ☐ **Standing water below building.** Ponding below a building is a red flag condition and usually warrants attention by a licensed geotechnical engineer. Unless the moisture source is faulty plumbing, site drainage improvements are typically needed.

Seasonal ground water has eroded soil, undermining structural pier below building.

Faulty site drainage causes ponding below building with potential for structural damage and other adverse effects.

6. ☐ **Sump pumps on property.** Sump pumps indicate that past drainage problems have occurred. The question is whether the sump pumps represent professional repairs, based upon evaluation by a geotechnical engineer, or attempted repairs by nonprofessionals. When pumps are found, confirmation of adequate drainage repair is recommended.

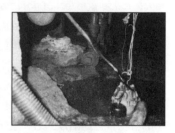

Sump pump indicates past or continuing drainage problems.

7. ☐ **Vapor barrier below building.** A vapor barrier typically consists of a plastic membrane installed on the ground surface below a building where ground moisture exists. The purpose of the membrane is to prevent evaporation, which can lead to moisture condensation on the structure. Where vapor barriers are observed, further evaluation of ground drainage conditions may be warranted, or additional ventilation may be needed. However, in some areas of the country, vapor barriers are required.

ASK THE $\mathcal{QA}$ INSPECTOR

Condensation and All That Rot

Dear Barry,

My house is being sold, and the buyer's home inspector found a major water problem under the building. The ground is muddy, droplets of water are hanging from the floor joists, and the wood is rotted. I checked under my neighbor's house to see if he has the same problem. His soil is also wet, but his floor framing is completely dry. Why am I having this problem when he is not?

Jason

Dear Jason,

Ground moisture beneath homes is a common problem in many areas. Typical causes include geological conditions, faulty grading of the lot, and overwatering of the landscaping. Sometimes, excessive watering at one property can cause flooding beneath a nearby home, especially in hillside areas.

To prevent moisture damage to the wood subfloor structure, the building code requires cross ventilation of the subarea. When vents are not provided, humidity from ground moisture may condense on the wood framing, as noted beneath your home. Prolonged moisture on wood members inevitably leads to fungus damage, commonly known as dryrot.

The minimum requirement for ventilation is 1 square foot of vent opening for each 150 square feet of floor area in the home. Where vent openings cannot be installed, the code requires a plastic membrane on the ground beneath the building to prevent the air in the subarea from becoming humid. In some cases, mechanical vents are needed.

In all likelihood, your neighbor's subarea is properly vented, while the space beneath your home probably is not. To ensure adequate ventilation, have the building checked by a licensed general contractor. To address the rotted framing, the structure should be thoroughly evaluated by a licensed pest control operator (commonly known as a termite inspector). It would also be wise to have the subarea evaluated for possible mold infestation.

---

8. ☐ **Soil erosion under or near building.** Evidence of soil erosion indicates past or recurrent problems with surface water flow and warrants further evaluation and drainage improvement.

9. ☐ **Faulty grade level at walls of building.** The soil and pavement against a building should not be in contact with siding or be above the level of the foundation. The grade level should also not be at or above the level of the stucco weep screed (a metal strip that forms the bottom of the stucco). Vio-

lations in this regard can cause moisture damage to buildings and infestation by wood-destroying organisms.

Soil erosion below building has undermined a portion of the foundation.

Concrete lacks required clearance below stucco weep screed.

10. ☐ **Raised planters against building.** Faulty grade levels against a building can result from adjacent planters that lack proper moisture protection for the building. Moisture protection may consist of an airspace between the planter and building or a substantial waterproof membrane.

11. ☐ **Water stains on basement walls.** Stains on basement walls indicate past or recurrent ground water problems. Where such stains are observed, further evaluation is warranted.

Ground moisture in planter can cause internal damage to wall.

White efflorescence on basement wall indicates gradual ground water seepage.

12. ☐ **Cracked or uneven slab.** Damage to concrete slabs can be caused by expansive clay soil, tree roots, excessive ground water, instability of the building site, or substandard construction. Symptoms should be reviewed and evaluated by a structural or geotechnical engineer.

Major crack in slab warrants evaluation by a licensed engineer.

ELECTRICAL CHECKLIST

The vast majority of homes have at least one electrical defect, but usually several are waiting to be found. Even in homes that are well-built and in which the electrical system is in generally good condition, some problems are likely to be discovered when the system is examined closely. Given the obvious safety implications of electrical defects, these are among the most important aspects of a home inspection. With this foundational understanding, the following conditions are among those most commonly considered by home inspectors:

Main Service Lines

These are the power supply lines from the utility company to the property.

Underground lines. Electric service lines to a building are often located below ground; inspection of such lines is obviously not possible. Home inspectors typically identify buried lines in their reports and indicate that they are not within the scope of the inspection. Defects involving underground lines, however, are usually rare.

Overhead lines. The following are the most common service line defects that your home inspector is likely to find:

1. ☐ **Damaged wire insulation.** The protective insulation on service lines can be damaged for various reasons; the most common cause being prolonged weather exposure. On old power lines, the insulation can be cracked and crumbling, resulting in exposed live wires. Movement of these wires could bring them into contact, with adverse and momentous consequences.

Service lines are within reach of any kid who can climb a chain-link fence.

2. ☐ **Damaged mast.** The service mast is the vertical pipe, extending above the roof, where the power lines enter the building. A damaged mast may compromise the secure attachment of the power lines and can promote rain intrusion into the service panel.

Service mast is leaning due to rust damage at base.

3. ☐ **Bare connectors at the mast.** Utility companies attach their service lines with special connecting hardware near the mast. The protective tape on old-style connectors tends to deteriorate with prolonged exposure to the weather, resulting in exposed live metal surfaces. Retaping of these connections is occasionally needed.

4. ☐ **No drip loop at the mast.** The drip loop is a U-shaped bend in the service wires just before they enter the mast. This bend prevents rain water from draining into the mast and down into the service panel.

5. ☐ **Lines too close to the roof.** Electric wires in contact with roof surfaces can scrape against abrasive roofing materials during windy weather, eroding the insulation, exposing the live wires and posing shock hazards and the potential for fire. Wires may be too low because of a short mast or because the utility company needs to adjust the slack in the lines.

Substandard service lines on this roof constitute an electrician's nightmare.

6. ☐ **Lines too close to the ground.** Overhead wires are required to be at least 10 feet above ground and 12 feet above a driveway. Power companies, unfortunately, have different minimum height standards than those in the National Electric Code, posing some confusion in determining when lines are actually in violation. The main point, however, is that lines too close to the ground are within reach of yard tools, sticks, pipes, and other objects that might be in the hands of workers or children at play.

7. ☐ **Lines too close to a driveway.** Low wires above driveways can interfere with the passage of large vehicles such as moving vans. Impact with these lines can produce undesired results.

8. ☐ **Lines in contact with trees.** Service lines often pass through nearby trees. Limbs sometimes bear heavily on lines, and wind movement of branches can cause damage to the insulation. Pruning tree limbs is the most common solution, and utility companies often (but not always) perform this work.

Tree branches are in contact with main service lines and should be reviewed by power company.

9. ☐ **Lines too small for the service panel.** This is an uncommon defect, occurring where the service panel on an older home has been upgraded without concurrent upgrading of the old, low-capacity service lines. Where this condition exists, the utility company should be notified.

Breaker Panels and Fuse Panels

The list of faulty conditions potentially lurking in residential electric panels is almost limitless. The following roster, therefore, although formidable, contains only the most likely defects to be reported by a home inspector:

10. ☐ **Fuses versus circuit breakers.** In pre-1950 homes, low capacity, fused systems are common, and home inspectors are likely to recommend upgrading to modern capacity systems equipped with circuit breakers. Panel replacement is a rather costly process and not legally mandated in most municipalities. Insurance companies, however, are often unwilling to write fire policies for properties with fused panels and may insist upon panel replacement as a precondition to providing coverage.

Fuses are repeatedly replaced in this old panel, indicating frequent overloading. Some people make the mistake of installing higher capacity fuses, as observed in the photo at right.

In this panel, 30 amp fuses have been installed at 20 amp circuits. This is a fire hazard. Also noted in this photo is double-tapping at the middle circuit.

11. ☐ **Double-tapping.** A common defect in many electric panels is the attachment of two wires to one circuit breaker or fuse terminal. Some breakers are designed to accommodate two separate wires, but most are not. When two wires are attached to a connector that is designed for one wire, the degree of contact between the wires and connector can be compromised, resulting in overheated connections. Double-tapping is also an indication that someone without adequate electrical knowledge has modified the system— a suspicion that warrants evaluation by a licensed electrical contractor.

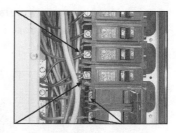

The upper two arrows indicate double-tapping, the installation of two wires at one terminal. The lower arrows indicate overfusing, with 30 amp wires connected to 40 amp breakers. This is a fire hazard.

12. ☐ **Overfusing.** A common finding by home inspectors is overfusing— where the capacity of the breaker or fuse exceeds the capacity of the wire. If that sounds too complicated, the simple explanation is that it is a significant fire hazard. If too much power is drawn on that circuit (a condition known as overload), the breaker or fuse will not disconnect, and the wire will then overheat. In most cases, the solution is to downsize the breaker or fuse.

13. ☐ **Missing handle ties at 240-volt circuits.** Two separate breakers are typically required for 240-volt circuits. The switch handles for these pairs of breakers must be joined together with connecting hardware so that an overload at one breaker will cause both breakers to be turned off. Without a handle tie, an overloaded 240-volt circuit would not be fully turned off by the breakers.

Lower panel is not designed for exterior use. Lack of a weatherproof exterior cover enables moisture intrusion.

14. ☐ **Damaged panel covers.** The purpose of the panel cover is to protect the live components from accidental contact, particularly by children. Panel covers can be damaged by weather exposure or by mishandling or modification by unqualified handypersons. Damaged covers should be repaired or replaced as needed.

15. ☐ **Missing panel covers.** When panel covers are missing, live electrical components are exposed to contact by children. Immediate replacement is recommended.

Panel cover replacement is substandard: roughly fabricated from thin gauge sheet metal.

The panel cover was discarded to enable installation of an added circuit. The hazards of exposed components are magnified by the panel's proximity to a hot tub, as shown in the photo below.

Not a great place for kids.

16. ☐ **Unprotected panel openings.** Panel covers have knockout openings—small rectangular popouts—to provide spaces for installing circuit breakers. Some panels have open knockouts that contain no breakers; these openings can be enticing to the inquisitive fingers of children. Special snap-on caps are available for added safety.

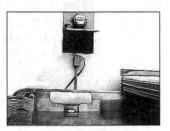

Open panel knockouts need protective covers.

17. ☐ **Corroded terminals.** Rust and corrosion can occur on wire connections at breakers and in fuse panels. Common causes are weather exposure, leakage at the mast, or aluminum connections without antioxidant. Corrosion can reduce conductivity at the connections, causing overheating of the wires.

18. ☐ **Taped wire splices.** Spliced wire connections should be fastened and protected with hardware specifically designed for that purpose. Electrical tape is a temporary means of covering bare wire ends, because the sticky surface eventually dries out and loses its adhesion. Taped splices in an electric panel indicate that wiring was modified by an unqualified handyperson.

Major corrosion is apparent at breaker terminals.

Taped wire splices in main panel.

19. ☐ **No main shutoff device.** A main service panel that has more than six breakers must have a single switch for turning off the main power to the system. Violations are often found in older homes, where the service panel originally had six or fewer circuits but where more circuits were subsequently added.

20. ☐ **Substandard service capacity.** The minimum required size for a main service panel is based upon the actual power demands of the residence. An electrical system in a modern home might simultaneously feed power to 20 lights, a toaster, a bathroom exhaust fan, an air conditioner, a hair dryer, a stereo, two computers, and more. In an older home, vintage 1940, the capacity of the system might only be adequate for 6 lights, a refrigerator, and a radio. Although modernization of older systems is not mandated, home inspectors typically recommend upgrading, and insurance companies may insist upon it.

Overdue for a new service panel.

ASK THE INSPECTOR

Aluminum Wire Fire Hazard

Dear Barry,

As a veteran Realtor, I've had many clients who shy away from homes with aluminum wiring. The home inspectors I know always raise a "red flag" when aluminum wire is found, and I'd like to know how this issue should be approached. When is aluminum a problem, and is it ever OK?

Carol

Dear Carol,

Aluminum wire is widely regarded as a significant fire hazard. Installed as 120-volt wiring in homes and mobile homes from the late 1960s through the early 1970s, it is routinely disclosed by home inspectors and warrants careful attention whenever found.

Problems with aluminum wires occur primarily at the connections. Fittings often become loose, resulting in overheating, carbon buildup, and eventual fire inside the walls. Gradual melting and smoldering of the wire insulation may sometimes occur for years before a fire actually ignites. Because of this, a detailed evaluation by a licensed electrical contractor is necessary to ensure that the entire electrical system is safe.

A proper evaluation includes an inspection of all connections in the breaker panels and at every outlet, switch, light fixture, and junction box in the building. This is obviously a very time-consuming (and therefore costly) process, but that is obviously preferable to the risk of a fire.

A common misconception is the belief that aluminum wiring must be replaced. This is an overreaching solution to a problem that merely requires modification of the connections. A qualified electrician can upgrade the wire ends so that the problems associated with aluminum are sufficiently eliminated. For specific details in this regard, consult a licensed electrical contractor.

21. ☐ **Aluminum wiring.** Aluminum wiring
is currently used for 240-volt stranded cables.
This is acceptable if the connectors are rated
for aluminum wire and if the wire ends are
treated with antioxidant. From the late 1960s
through the early 1970s, aluminum was also
installed for 120-volt circuits in many homes,
but this use was abandoned when loose aluminum connections were found to cause
fires. When home inspectors encounter 120-
volt aluminum wiring, the standard recom-

Corrosion on aluminum wire ends can reduce conductivity and cause overheating of wires.

mendation is that all connections at the panels, outlets, lights, switches, and
other fixtures be fully reviewed and upgraded by a licensed electrical contractor. Satisfactory upgrades can usually be made without rewiring the dwelling.

22. ☐ **Burned wires.** Burned insulation or
blackened wire ends obviously indicate that
wires have overheated. Common causes are
loose connections, substandard aluminum
connections, or breakers that failed to trip
when there was a circuit overload. These are
fire hazards warranting immediate attention
by a licensed electrical contractor.

All neutral wires are burned. This panel poses a major fire hazard.

23. ☐ **Faulty grounding.** Entire books have
been written about the finer points of proper
electrical grounding. Most of this information
is well beyond the understanding of those
not professionally acquainted with electrical
wiring. Among the more common violations
found in panels are the lack of bonding at
ground busses, loose clamps at ground rods
and water lines, substandard ground connections in panels, combined ground and neutral
wires at subpanels, bonded neutral busses in

The main ground wire for this service panel has been severed.

subpanels, and so on. All such conditions are typically reported by home inspectors and warrant attention by a licensed electrician.

24. ☐ **Innumerable miscellaneous conditions.** Home inspectors routinely anticipate the foregoing conditions. A far lengthier list would include defects
that are less common; that an inspector might see only once in a career. The
conditions that result from unqualified persons modifying electrical wiring are
limitless. Even without faulty wiring, the safety of an electrical panel can become compromised. For example, a home inspector removed a panel cover

and found that the breaker box was completely filled with acorns, courtesy of the neighborhood squirrel. Another inspector discovered within a panel the deceased remains of an ill-fated snake.

This substandard outlet, added to a breaker panel by some daring handyperson, is an open invitation to summary electrocution.

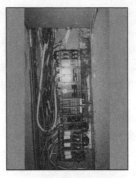

For purposes of electrical safety, it is recommended that decomposing remnants of the late rat at the right side of this panel be carefully exhumed by a qualified electrician.

Wiring Problems

This section addresses faulty wiring in such areas as attics, crawlspaces, closets, eaves, decks, garages, or anywhere that wiring is not concealed within the construction or buried beneath the ground. Commonly reported conditions include:

25. ☐ **Knob and tube wiring.** The earliest form of residential wiring is commonly called "knob and tube," named for the ceramic insulators used to secure the wires to the wood framing. It was commonly installed until approximately 1950. Knob and tube wiring is not inherently unsafe, but it is substandard for several reasons: it lacks ground wiring; it typically does not include sufficient numbers of circuits for contemporary use; and burial beneath attic insulation can cause overheating of the wires. Upgrading is generally not mandatory, but home inspectors typically advise it, and fire insurance companies sometimes demand it.

An example of old knob and tube wiring. The coffee can indicates roof leaking above the junction box. Further evaluation of the roof is warranted.

26. ☐ **Exposed wiring.** Wiring that is not enclosed and protected within the construction
of a building or buried beneath the ground
should be contained in piping, known as
"conduit," to prevent accidental damage to
the insulation. When wires are installed by
homeowners or handypersons, exposed wiring is often the result.

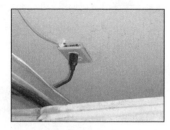

*This is an example of substandard
wiring, installed by an amateur.*

27. ☐ **Substandard conduit.** The electrical
code specifies materials that are approved
for use as wire conduit. Unapproved materials, such as polyvinyl chloride
(PVC) water pipe, are identified as substandard by home inspectors.

*White PVC water pipe was used as
electrical conduit. Damage is due to
inappropriate location.*

*Glaring example of attic wiring
installed by someone other than a
qualified electrician.*

28. ☐ **Exposed wire splices.** A common indication of nonprofessional wiring
is exposed wire splices. Typically, these appear as wire ends twisted together
and covered with tape or wire nuts. All such connections should be contained in protective enclosures, known as "junction boxes."

29. ☐ **Junction boxes without covers.** All junction boxes should have covers to protect the
wire splices contained in them. Omitted box
covers are common in attics, garages, and in
subareas below buildings.

30. ☐ **Junction boxes without wire grommets.**
Junction boxes have knockout holes for in-
serting wires. Because the edges of these
holes are sharp and can cut through wire insulation, wire grommets are specifically de-

*Junction boxes in attic lack cover
plates and are not secured to
framing.*

signed to prevent this kind of damage and are required at junction box
openings. This also applies where wires enter breaker panels and fuse boxes.

31. ☐ **Exposed wire ends.** Disconnected or abandoned wire ends are some-times left dangling, without regard to shock hazards or fire hazards. Termi-nated wire ends should be capped with wire nuts and contained within junction boxes, or they should be entirely removed.

Romex wires enter opening in breaker panel without protective hardware. Wire insulation is exposed to sharp metal edge.

Disconnected wire ends should be safely terminated to prevent untoward consequences.

32. ☐ **Exposed wiring in garages.** When wiring is installed horizontally in the open framing of unfinished garage walls, it must be at least seven feet above the floor. Exposed horizontal wiring at lower levels can be used to hang ob-jects such as tools and is therefore prohibited. Other wiring problems are also common to garages, as this part of the building often serves as the testing ground for self-appointed jacks of all trades.

Typical example of "Handy Andy" garage wiring.

A typical example of dastardly daredevil wiring.

33. ☐ **Innumerable miscellaneous conditions.** The foregoing conditions are those most commonly reported by home inspectors. A complete list of po-tential defects would include every conceivable example of improper wiring to which unqualified persons are likely to resort. That list could fill another volume.

Outlets and Lights

This section addresses faulty conditions involving lights, switches, and outlets. Defects in this category are so common that most homes harbor at least one. Commonly reported conditions include:

34. ☐ **Two-prong outlets.** Homes built in the early 1960s or prior typically contain two-prong outlets. These are the old style of wall outlets—not equipped with a ground receptacle. Home inspectors routinely point these out as obsolete, but replacement in most areas is not required. However, where computers and other electronic devices are installed, grounded outlets are advised, as they are needed for proper function of surge suppressors.

An old damaged two-prong outlet: particularly unsafe for children.

35. ☐ **Miscellaneous outlet defects such as:**
- *Lack of ground*
- *Reversed hot and neutral*
- *Reversed hot and ground*
- *Open neutral connection*
- *Defective ground fault devices.*

Most home inspectors use a test device that they plug into accessible wall outlets. Receptacles that are not readily accessible, such as those behind furniture, are not tested. Buyers often assume that this test is to determine whether each outlet is working. Actually, the tester can determine the existence of several faulty conditions, as noted above. Some inspectors use more sophisticated testers that check for voltage variations and other esoteric inconsistencies.

Exposed live terminal at damaged outlet is extremely hazardous to children. Immediate replacement is warranted.

36. ☐ **Lack of ground fault protection.** Outlets subject to moisture exposure require protection by means of ground fault circuit interrupters (GFCIs). Those who have no idea what a GFCI outlet is may recall having seen bathroom outlets with two built-in buttons, usually a red and a black. GFCI outlets provide protection from electric shock and are required for exterior outlets and those in bathrooms, garages, kitchens, laundries, and near

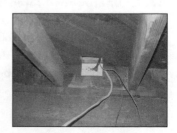

Mystery GFCI outlet in subarea provides power to who knows what. This Instance incorporates several electrical code violations.

pools, spas, wet bars, and other sinks. With each new version of the National Electrical Code, more locations are added to this list.

ASK THE INSPECTOR

Do GFCI Outlets Have to Be Grounded?

Dear Barry,

A home inspector suggested that I replace the ungrounded outlets in my bathroom with GFCI outlets for added safety. He explained that GFCI outlets can prevent electric shock where appliances are used near water. My contractor disagrees. He says that GFCI outlets will not work with my old wiring system because there are no ground wires. Is there any way to add GFCI protection to my bathroom outlets without the extra expense of installing ground wires?

Dave

Dear Dave,

The home inspector's advice is correct. Grounding is not necessary for proper function of a GFCI (ground fault circuit interrupter). These outlets function by detecting differences in amperage between the hot and neutral wires. When these amp levels are not equal, the GFCI device assumes there is a safety problem and promptly disconnects the power, with or without a ground.

GFCI outlets require hot and neutral wires only. In older homes, where ground wires are not installed, GFCI outlets can significantly improve safety at very minimal cost. They are recommended not only at the bathroom outlets but also outlets at the kitchen, laundry, wet bar, garage, pool, spa, exterior, and any other place where electricity is likely to be used near water.

———————————

37. ☐ **Ungrounded three-prong outlets.** In older homes, originally wired with two-prong outlets, three-prong outlets have often been installed as an "upgrade" by handypersons. Unfortunately, most of these homes do not have ground wires as part of the outlet circuitry. Consequently, the added three-prong outlets appear to be grounded when, in fact, they are not.

38. ☐ **Missing or damaged cover plates.** Outlets and switches should be properly covered to prevent exploratory excursions by juvenile fingers.

Outlet should have been shielded from texture spray. Overspray on internal contacts affects safety of fixture.

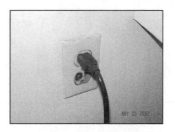

Burnt outlet is subject to internal damage and should be replaced.

39. ☐ **Outlets with scorch marks.** Burn marks on an outlet indicate an occurrence that may have damaged the internal components of the fixture. Professional evaluation and replacement of such outlets is recommended.

40. ☐ **Inoperative outlets.** Outlets are occasionally found to have no power. Because numerous potential causes can explain an apparent lack of power, further evaluation is usually needed.

41. ☐ **Electrical devices near tubs and showers.** Outlets and switches are often installed within reach of tubs and showers—an impractical arrangement for obvious safety reasons, but not legally prohibited. Upgrading is advised but not required.

42. ☐ **Lack of weather protection.** Weatherproof covers are required for exterior outlets and switches, but they are sometimes omitted or damaged. Lack of weather protection can cause moisture damage to the internal components.

Metallic light fixtures should not be installed above tubs or showers.

43. ☐ **Attic insulation on ceiling lights.** Recessed ceiling lights are often covered with attic insulation. Some fixtures are rated for coverage with insulation but others are not. When insulation is installed over lights not rated for coverage, overheating can result.

Exterior outlet needs a weather resistant cover.

Attic insulation can cause recessed light fixture to overheat.

ASK THE INSPECTOR

Ceiling Lights May Have Heat Damage

Dear Barry,

The recessed lights in my kitchen ceiling have been flickering for years, but I never did anything about it. Now that I'm selling the property, the home inspector says the lights were covered with insulation in the attic, causing them to overheat. He removed the insulation, but this didn't eliminate the flickering. What do you suggest I do?

Pat

Dear Pat,

It is fortunate that this condition was finally discovered. Canister lights should have unrestricted air exposure to promote adequate cooling. Covering them with insulation causes overheating, and this can pose a serious fire hazard. Some of the newer model lights do not have this problem—that is, they will not overheat if covered with insulation—but yours are apparently older vintage.

The persistent flickering of the lights should have alerted you to the need for professional evaluation. Malfunctioning electric fixtures should never be ignored. The fact that flickering has continued after the insulation was removed indicates that the fixtures or wire connections have suffered damage from prolonged heat exposure. The solution is immediate review by a licensed electrician.

44. ☐ **Loose or damaged light fixtures.** Loose light fixtures should be securely fastened, especially exterior lights that are prone to rain intrusion. Damaged fixtures should be repaired or replaced as needed.

Closet light fixture is improperly installed and constitutes a fire hazard.

45. ☐ **Lack of essential lighting.** Lighting should be provided at all exits to promote safe egress for those leaving the building at night. Light switches are also needed at room entrances. These may be wired to built-in light fixtures or to wall outlets.

46. ☐ **Lack of essential outlets.** In newer buildings, an outlet is required for every six linear feet of wall. Older homes require fewer outlets, and very old homes typically have very few. Additional outlets are advised but generally not required for older homes.

47. ☐ **Ceiling fans with light dimmers.** Homeowners often install light dimmers on ceiling fan-light fixtures to enable dimming of the lights and controlling the fan speed. Unfortunately, light dimmers (known as "rheostats") operate by reducing voltage, which is damaging to motors. Humming is an indication that the motor has already been adversely affected. A proper speed-control device (known as a "varitrol switch") operates by reducing the cycles of the alternating current without changing the voltage.

48. ☐ **Innumerable miscellaneous conditions.** The possibilities for substandard installations of outlets, lights, and other fixtures is limited only by the collective imaginations of homeowners and handypersons attempting to perform electrical repairs, alterations, and modifications.

This light fixture becomes a fish bowl during rainy weather.

PLUMBING CHECKLIST

Plumbing conditions are among the most crucial considerations of a home inspection because repairs are often costly, and the consequences of faulty plumbing can include moisture damage or mold infestation. With this in mind, the following aspects of a plumbing system are routinely considered during a home inspection:

Main Water Line

Concealed portion of main line. Main water supply lines, in large part, are buried beneath the ground and are therefore not within the scope of a home inspection. If a main line is old galvanized steel, it is likely to be rusted and could have limited remaining life, but this cannot be determined without excavating portions of the pipe.

Visible portion of main line. The portion of the main line that enters the building is often visible at the exterior of the structure and is usually where the main shutoff valve is installed. Home inspectors typically check this portion of the main line for the following:

1. ☐ **Physical defects.** Common visible defects in the main water line include actual damage (possibly due to impact), corrosion (such as rust where the pipe contacts the ground), and leakage at faulty or corroded fittings.

2. ☐ **Undersized pipe diameter.** The minimum required inside pipe diameter for a domestic water supply line is ¾ inch. For homes with greater water supply needs, larger supply piping may be required.

3. ☐ **Damaged shutoff valve.** Damage to main supply valves usually involves corrosion—sometimes visible, sometimes internal. Corrosion within the valve typically renders the fixture incapable of turning off the water supply. Home inspectors generally test the valve to verify that it is operable.

4. ☐ **Leaking shutoff valve.** Steady dripping occurs at some valves due to corrosion or faulty seals. Sometimes a valve that has not been operated for many years will begin to leak if the handle is turned.

5. ☐ **Inaccessible shutoff valve.** A main shutoff valve should be fully accessible in case of a plumbing emergency. Some valves are buried and need ground clearance; some are pressed against a wall, preventing the handle from being turned; and many are engulfed in overgrown foliage.

ASK THE INSPECTOR

Every Home Needs a Separate Water Shutoff

Dear Barry,

Our condominium complex was built in the early 1990s, and we have already experienced several plumbing problems. That wouldn't be so bad if each condo had its own water supply shutoff valve. Whenever a leak occurs at one unit, the water to all units must be turned off while repairs are in progress. Our owners association requested that separate valves be provided, but we were told that this is not required by code. What should we do?

Roger

Dear Roger,

Someone is pulling the collective leg of your condo association membership. The Uniform Plumbing Code specifically requires "that supply piping to a single family residence . . . be controlled on one valve." If your condo complex does not have a separate water supply valve for each living unit, then the builder messed up, and the building inspector failed to identify the problem prior to approving the project. If the persons responsible for this mistake are not convinced that separate valves are mandated, have them read section 605.2 of the plumbing code. (If they're using the old code, that's section 1005(b).)

6. ☐ **Lack of a shutoff valve.** Older homes (circa 1960s or earlier) often lack a main shutoff valve except at the utility service meter. Although upgrading is usually not a legal requirement, it is recommended that a main valve be added to allow emergency water shutoff by the homeowner.

Water Piping within the Building

The internal water supply system of a home is largely concealed within the construction and is therefore not accessible for inspection, especially in homes that are built on slab foundations. Nevertheless, a number of significant defects are discernible by qualified home inspectors. Conditions likely to be disclosed are as follows:

7. ☐ **Evidence of internal corrosion.** Copper piping, the material of choice since the late 1960s, is generally not prone to significant internal corrosion. Problems due to rust and deterioration are common with galvanized steel piping, commonly found in older homes.

Major corrosion of galvanized pipe fittings is sometimes caused by interaction of dissimilar metals.

8. ☐ **Restricted water flow.** Reduced water volume can occur when two or more plumbing fixtures are in use at the same time and is a telltale symptom of internal corrosion within the pipes. Those who shower in older homes can attest to this (e.g., "Don't flush the toilet, I'm in the shower!"). The solution is repiping.

9. ☐ **Leaking at connections.** Leaking at pipe fittings can be due to poorly secured fittings, rusted galvanized pipe, excessive water pressure, and the like. Once disclosed by a home inspector, the next step is evaluation and repairs by a licensed plumber.

Slow leaking is occurring at rusted pipe fittings. System needs repiping.

10. ☐ **Inadequate support of pipes.** Piping below a building may lack adequate support. Rather than being strapped to the floor framing, it may sag or be in contact with the soil, often an indication that plumbing was installed by unqualified nonprofessionals.

11. ☐ **Excessive water pressure.** Homeowners often think there's no such thing as too much pressure. They confuse good strong water flow with high pressure. Actually, good flow is a function of pipe diameter and condition, not pressure. Excess pressure can actually be undesirable: it can separate connections in a dishwasher or a toilet supply line, causing flooding of a home.

12. ☐ **Copper/galvanized steel contact.** Copper pipes and galvanized steel pipes should never be in direct contact. When copper meets steel in a water supply line, electrolysis occurs, causing accelerated corrosion. To prevent damage to the pipes, dielectric fittings are required.

Connecting copper pipe to galvanized steel pipes promotes internal corrosion. Proper connections are shown in the photo at right.

The brass pipe serves as a dielectric fitting between the copper and galvanized steel pipes, preventing electrolysis and corrosion.

13. ☐ **Water supply connected to drain line.** Direct connections between wastewater drains and water supply lines are strictly prohibited. The plumbing code restricts such connections because they can cause contamination of the water supply. A common violation is connection of a water softener discharge pipe to a sewer line.

Water softener discharge pipe is connected to waste line. Backflow could contaminate water supply.

14. ☐ **Unapproved types of water piping.** The plumbing code lists all of the piping materials that are approved for use in a water supply system. Materials not on that list are prohibited for such use.

15. ☐ **Asbestos insulation on water piping.** In old homes, asbestos was sometimes used to insulate hot water piping. This type of asbestos material is often friable (crushable with hand pressure) and is therefore considered to be potentially hazardous.

16. ☐ **Innumerable miscellaneous conditions.** The numbers and kinds of plumbing defects likely to be found by home inspectors are limited only by the abilities of unqualified handypersons to devise "creative"new ways of installing pipes and other fixtures.

Homeowner's failed attempt to fabricate a new and unique water heater flue pipe connection.

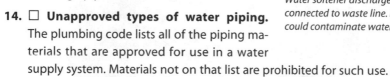

Waste Lines

This term refers to the drain piping that connects the plumbing fixtures to the sewer or septic system. In homes on slab foundations, most waste lines are not visible for inspection. Conditions commonly disclosed are as follows:

17. ☐ **Rusted cast iron drains.** Most cast iron drain pipes are very old, and because iron is not a rust-resistant material, damage due to corrosion is common. Replacement of these lines is often recommended.

18. ☐ **Leaking drains.** Drain leaks typically occur at loose or poorly sealed pipe fittings or where corrosion has produced holes in the pipe. Leaky fittings can usually be repaired, but leaking due to corrosion requires replacement of the deteriorated pipe.

Old cast iron drain pipe is cracked, rusted, and leaking.

19. ☐ **Drain without adequate slope.** Drain pipes must have a minimum degree of slope, as provided by code, to promote the flow of solid and liquid waste materials. Lack of adequate slope can cause congestion in the lines.

Leakage and resultant rust damage are apparent at kitchen sink drain.

Drain was apparently installed with the expectation that water flows uphill. Hint: Lines on foundation are level.

20. ☐ **Poorly vented or unvented drains.**
Drains must be vented in order to maintain
the water seal in drain traps and to prevent
sewer gases from entering the dwelling
through open drains in sinks and other fixtures.

*S-traps, such as these, are
prohibited because they are not
properly vented.*

21. ☐ **Clogged or restricted drains.** Drains obviously need free, unrestricted flow. Slow
draining can be due to congestion with foreign matter or faulty installation of the piping.
Inspectors often recommend further evaluation by a licensed plumber to determine the cause.

*Someone asked why the home
inspector did not test the sink
plumbing or inspect the counter.*

*Drain fitting separated because pipe
was not adequately strapped to
framing.*

22. ☐ **Inadequate support of drain pipes.** Drain piping beneath a building
must be securely fastened to the structure to prevent sagging from the
weight of water in the lines. Sagging drains can cause congestion due to solid
waste buildup in drooping portions of the lines.

23. ☐ **Faulty sink traps.** The U-shaped drain
pipe below a sink is known as a trap. Water re-
tained in the trap prevents sewer gases from
venting into the building. Some traps leak,
some are damaged, and some are installed
incorrectly.

*Hallucinogenic drain trap
installation.*

24. ☐ Innumerable miscellaneous conditions. As with water supply piping, there is no end to the list of potential problems with waste-line systems. So long as unqualified persons compete with professional plumbers, various forms of substandard drains will proliferate, challenging the forensic skills of home inspectors.

Shower drain pipe below floor was installed without a trap. Price tag on fitting indicates that work was not performed by a plumber.

ASK THE INSPECTOR

Verifying the Age of a Home

Dear Barry,

When we purchased our home, we were told that it was 15 years old, and the seller validated this by showing us the manufacture date in the toilet tank. Recently, while repairing a leak in the other toilet, we found a manufacture date that was 12 years older. Now we're wondering if the house is older than disclosed. How can we verify the age of our home?

Gwenn

Dear Gwenn,

In recent years, the presence of manufacture dates in toilet tanks has become common knowledge, and many people now rely on this information as verification of a building's age. Although the date in the water tank may coincide with the year a home was built, this method of dating a structure is not infallible and should not be regarded as a definite confirmation of vintage.

In some homes, the toilets are not the original fixtures. They may have been installed as replacements to facilitate water conservation, or they may have been part of a remodelling project or an addition. On the other hand, it is possible that a used toilet was installed when the home was new, giving the false impression that the building is older.

Other dated fixtures include gas connectors and furnaces, but their dates are also not wholly reliable and are sometimes difficult to discern.

The best way to verify a home's age is to check with the local building department or other municipal agencies for the permit history. If for any reason they cannot provide this information, consult the local tax assessor's office, whose records may show the year when the lot was reassessed as improved property.

Gas or Fuel Piping

Faulty plumbing involving fuel piping is obviously more serious than defective water piping. Leaking water can damage or destroy property. Leaking fuel can damage or destroy property and lives. Therefore, determining fuel-system defects is critically important when inspecting a home. In most areas of the country, fuel piping involves natural gas or liquid propane gas (LPG); in some regions, fuel piping is for heating oil. Conditions commonly disclosed are as follows:

25. ☐ **Rusted gas piping.** Gas line corrosion is typically the result of moisture exposure from one source or another. Such conditions require immediate attention to prevent fuel leakage and related consequences.

26. ☐ **Buried pipe without rust protection.** Buried fuel lines must have a rustproof surface to prevent corrosion and resultant leaks. Steel fuel piping should be plastic-coated or wrapped with a special waterproof tape. This rust protection is mandatory, not only for buried pipe, but for any lines within 6 inches of grade.

Buried gas piping lacks rust preventive coating.

27. ☐ **Odor of leaking gas.** Inspectors should always be attentive to odors that would indicate gas leaks at pipes, valves, or fixtures. When leaks are detected, the gas supply company should be notified immediately.

28. ☐ **Copper gas piping.** Copper is not approved for natural gas piping because trace amounts of sulfur in natural gas can corrode copper. Some older homes (circa 1950s) were plumbed with copper gas pipes. These lines may be tin-lined, which would prevent adverse effects from sulfur, but the lining cannot be determined unless the fittings are separated to enable inspection. Copper gas piping warrants further evaluation by a licensed plumber or the gas supply company.

Someone added copper tubing at meter as a supply line to a barbecue.

29. ☐ **Gas connectors through construction.** Flex connectors, the short corrugated pipes used to connect gas-burning fixtures, may not legally pass through a wall, floor, cabinet, appliance casing, or other partition. Where violations are found, the addition of rigid gas piping is needed.

30. ☐ **Main shutoff valve at building.** Every building should have a main gas shutoff valve for emergency use by the occupants. Some dwellings are not equipped with a shutoff that is reasonably accessible. In such cases, upgrading is strongly recommended.

31. ☐ **Gas piping embedded in concrete.** Where gas piping emerges from the ground, paving should not be installed in direct contact with the pipe. Clearance should be provided so that movement of the pavement for any reason will not cause stress or damage to the gas pipe.

32. ☐ **Gas-pipe unions within a building.** The use of pipe unions is prohibited where gas piping is contained within a structure. Yet because many building departments do not enforce this code, unions can be found in the majority of subareas beneath buildings. Fortunately, leaking almost never occurs at these unions; therefore, home in-

Pavement is installed in contact with supply pipe to gas service meter.

spectors will often point them out as noncomplying but will not stress the need for upgrading.

33. ☐ **Protection of gas meters.** Gas meters installed near streets or driveways must have protection from vehicle impact. Where meters are exposed to damage by vehicles, steel posts (known as bollards) or masonry barricades should be firmly placed as a means of protection.

Steel barricade installed to protect gas meter from vehicle impact.

34. ☐ **PVC plastic gas pipe.** Synthetic gas piping is limited to specifically approved materials, for burial only, and this does not include polyvinyl chloride (PVC). Yellow PVC was formerly approved for this use, but has now been disallowed. Wherever plastic gas pipe is subject to question, evaluation by a licensed plumber is recommended. The most commonly used and approved material is yellow polyethylene.

Would-be plumbers are installing PVC water pipe as a new gas main.

35. ☐ **Inadequate support of gas pipes.** Gas pipes should be securely attached to the structure, especially in a subarea, where lack of secure attachment could result in ground contact and resultant rust damage.

Gas supply pipe lacks adequate support.

36. ☐ **Undersized gas piping.** The minimum required diameter of a gas pipe is determined by its length and the British thermal unit (BTU) demand of the fixtures being served. Undersizing of gas piping can pose safety hazards due to the lack of adequate gas flow to burners.

37. ☐ **Innumerable miscellaneous conditions.** So long as handypersons deem themselves qualified to confront the hazards of gas pipe installation and modification, the list of potential gas-related problems will be endless. Examples include garden hose or aquarium hose used as gas piping, gas valves enclosed within walls, and on and on.

Gas connector to furnace consists of rigid aluminum, rather than flex, and is installed through furnace casing, with connection concealed in wall, and with no apparent gas shutoff valve. Aside from that, it's an excellent installation.

Heavier-Than-Air Gas

Liquid propane gas (LPG) is a common fuel source in rural areas. Because LPG is heavier than air, it is more hazardous than natural gas and is therefore subject to special considerations. Conditions commonly disclosed by home inspectors are the following:

38. ☐ **Unprotected fuel tank near driveway.** Propane gas tanks installed near driveways or roadways need protection from vehicle impact; steel posts or a masonry wall are typical for this purpose. If a car or truck were to strike and rupture a propane tank, the resultant explosion could leave a crater the size of an Olympic-sized swimming pool.

If liquid propane gas tank had been installed near a driveway or roadway, protection from vehicle impact would have been required.

39. ☐ **Propane fixtures in a basement.** Propane fixtures are prohibited in basements unless there is a floor drain that can be piped downward to an exterior location. In some areas, propane is allowed in a basement if the supply line is equipped with a gas sensor and automatic shutoff valve. Propane leakage in a basement would create a vast reservoir of combustible gas; when ignited, this could convert a residence into a building site for an underground garage.

40. ☐ **Overflow pan under attic furnace.** Many building departments do not require an overflow pan when a propane-burning furnace is installed in an attic—an unfortunate oversight in the building code. In the event of a propane leak in an attic, the heavy gas would settle into the ceiling framing, rather than venting out of the building; the result could be a fire or an explosion. Recognizing this problem, some heating contractors install overflow pans, but, unfortunately, many do not. Upgrading is not required, but home inspectors should point out the inherent hazards wherever this condition is found.

41. ☐ **Propane gas in a fireplace.** In most areas, propane use in fireplaces is not prohibited, another unfortunate safety oversight. If a fireplace propane valve is turned on but the burner is not lit, the gas flows onto the floor rather than venting up the chimney. For this reason, propane in a fireplace, although legal, should be pointed out by home inspectors as a potential safety problem.

Water Heaters

Of all the individual fixtures found in a home, the one with the longest list of potential defects is the water heater. In fact, the majority of all water heaters have at least one of these violations. Conditions commonly disclosed are the following:

42. ☐ **Inadequate strapping or no strapping.** Requirements for strapping water heaters apply only in areas with a significant likelihood of earthquakes (Seismic Zones #3 and #4). Homeowners (and many plumbers) are often not adequately versed in the finer points of proper strapping; and even some building departments could benefit from related tutoring. For these reasons, strapping violations are common.

43. ☐ **Raised platform in a garage.** A water heater in a garage must be elevated so that the pilot light or other source of spark or flame is at least 18 inches above the floor. This is to prevent ignition of combustible fumes in the event of a gasoline leak or spill.

Acceptable method of strapping: Fixture is secured from opposing directions with plumbers tape and is fastened with lag bolts and washers.

44. ☐ **Raised platform needs bracing.** The platform that supports a water heater in a garage must be reinforced and stable. Water heaters are extremely heavy, and movement can cause a wobbly platform to collapse, separating the water lines and the gas or electrical connections.

Water heater in garage is installed on a raised platform, with a bollard (post) to protect fixture from vehicle impact. However, strapping is inadequate.

Water heater is installed on garage floor with no raised platform. Pilot light could ignite gasoline fumes.

ASK THE INSPECTOR

Beware of Water Heater Exhaust

Dear Barry,

I'm planning to move my water heater from the hall closet to a small shed I've built against the back of my house. The shed is next to a bedroom window, and I'm wondering how to keep the combustion exhaust from blowing into the house when the window is open. How far from the window should I install the exhaust pipe?

Val

Dear Val,

A water heater's flue pipe should extend at least 12 inches above the roof line and should terminate no closer than 4 feet from an openable window. My advice, however, is to stop what you are doing and call a licensed plumber. There are more safety considerations affecting the installation of a water heater than just the exhaust system. Other vital requirements include gas piping, combustion air supply, fire clearances, pressure relief, earthquake strapping (if you live in a seismically active area), and more. Without specific knowledge of plumbing code requirements, you'd be well advised to delegate the project to a qualified expert.

45. ☐ Missing relief valve. Every water heater must be equipped with a temperature/pressure relief (TPR) valve to prevent an explosion in the event of an overheated tank. The lack of a TPR valve is a significant safety violation.

When the discharge pipe cannot be run to the exterior of the building, a Watts regulator, depicted here, can shut off the gas supply when the fixture is overheated.

TPR discharge pipe is missing, and corrosion on relief valve indicates slow leakage.

46. ☐ Missing discharge pipe. Every TPR valve must be piped to the exterior of the building or to an alternate approved location, such as a laundry drain. This is to prevent expelled steam and hot water from causing personal injury or property damage.

47. ☐ PVC plastic discharge pipe. The purpose of a TPR discharge pipe is to convey steam and extremely hot water; so the pipe should consist of heat-resistant material. PVC plastic, commonly misused for this purpose, is not rated as a conduit for hot water. Replacement with approved piping is recommended.

48. ☐ Rust flakes in the burner chamber. Excessive rust in the burner chamber indicates that the water heater is deteriorated due to age and may not be long for this world. Rust flakes on the burner itself can also interfere with proper gas combustion.

PVC is prohibited for use with hot water. Bar code stickers on fittings indicate that installation was not done by a licensed plumber.

49. ☐ Rusted water connections. Rusted fittings may indicate minor or major problems and should be reviewed by a licensed plumber.

50. ☐ **Leaking water connections.** Plumbing leaks need little explanation. Immediate attention by a licensed plumber is always warranted.

Leaking and corrosion are apparent at water supply connector.

Ongoing leakage and rust damage indicate that fixture is overdue for retirement.

51. ☐ **Rust damage at the casing.** Damage to a water heater's casing is not a significant problem in and of itself, but it may indicate other problems, such as internal leakage.

52. ☐ **Missing covers at burner chamber.** The burner access has two covers; the purpose of the inner cover is to prevent overheating of the exterior cover and escape of exhaust fumes. It is essential that both covers be in place.

53. ☐ **Faulty gas connections.** There are more wrong ways than right ways to install a gas connection. Faulty gas connections to a water heater include leaky fittings, flex connectors linked in series, flex connectors without slack, rigid gas connectors, gas valve at the wrong end of the connector, missing gas valves, inaccessible gas valves, and so on.

Rigid aluminum gas connector does not provide adequate flexibility in the event of movement.

54. ☐ **Faulty flue piping.** The flue is the exhaust pipe that conveys combustion gases from the burner to the exterior of the building. A defective flue can cause people to breathe noxious fumes. Therefore, proper flue conditions are essential. Examples of defects include separated fittings, lack of screws at fittings, damage from corrosion, lack of vertical rise, and more.

Disconnected flue pipe vents exhaust into dwelling. Holes indicate where screws formerly secured this connection.

55. ☐ **Flue contact with combustibles.** Flue pipes become hot and must therefore have minimum clearances from all combustible materials. Contact with wood framing in the attic, for example, constitutes a significant fire hazard. Violations of this kind are common.

Single wall flue pipe is in contact with combustible cellulose ceiling tile.

Lack of combustion air openings at this closet caused flame roll-out at burner access. Note soot marks.

56. ☐ **Inadequate combustion air supply.** Essential to safe gas combustion is having an adequate supply of air. Water heaters installed in an enclosed space, such as a closet, must have air openings that comply with specific code requirements.

57. ☐ **No water shutoff valve.** A water heater must have a water shutoff valve to enable repair or replacement of the fixture without turning off the entire water supply to the building.

58. ☐ **Innumerable miscellaneous conditions.** The ability of homeowners and handypersons to devise new and unique ways of improperly installing water heaters is a testament to American ingenuity.

Flue pipe termites near an openable window. Exhaust can vent into bedroom, and heat from flue outlet could ignite dry foliage.

Bathroom Plumbing

Water Closets (commonly known as toilets). Toilets are flush with possibilities for defective conditions. Among those commonly reported by home inspectors are the following:

59. ☐ **Loose attachment to floor.** The bolts that secure a toilet to the floor are often found to be loose. Movement at the base can damage the wax seal, resulting in leakage and a rotted floor.

60. ☐ **Leaking wax seal.** A leaking wax seal may or may not be caused by a loose toilet. Moisture can lead to fungus and dryrot damage to the subfloor and framing. An indication of moisture is discoloration of the floor vinyl. In homes with raised foundations, home inspectors also check for toilet leakage when crawling beneath the building.

Discolored floor vinyl and moisture damage at baseboard are caused by leaking wax seal at base of toilet.

61. ☐ **Leaking at the base of the tank.** Leakage at the tank occurs much less frequently than at the floor seal. A leaking tank may be caused by a loose or damaged seal, a loose water supply connection, or a crack in the tank itself.

62. ☐ **Loose attachment of the tank.** When tanks are not securely attached to the back of the bowl, leaking may occur. Tightening should be done by a qualified professional to prevent cracking the fixture.

A modern alternative to "paperwork."

Fixture is fully operative and serves an additional vital function not related to plumbing.

63. ☐ **Toilet does not flush properly.** If the handle must be held down until the flush process is completed, the tank flapper may need replacement. If the flush action is not adequate to remove waste from the bowl, there could be congestion in the drain line, or the toilet fixture may be poorly designed.

ASK THE INSPECTOR

Two Flush or Not Two Flush

Dear Barry,

We hired a home inspector, and he noted that one of the toilets has an unusual habit. When the flush handle is pressed, the toilet actually flushes twice. The water goes around and down, the bowl refills, and then it goes around and down again. The seller considers this a positive thing. What do you think?

Brian

Dear Brian,

This condition is technically a defect but not a significant problem. My guess is that this is a low-flow toilet with tank hardware that is faulty or out of adjustment. Low-flow toilets are designed to complete the flush action with a limited amount of water—approximately 1.6 gallons, according to their design specifications. The flush tank typically holds more water than this, but the tank hardware is designed to permit a limited portion of this water to flow into the bowl with each flush.

If this toilet is repeating the flush action with each use, the tank is probably releasing all of its contents into the bowl. After the initial flush performance is completed, water continues to flow from the tank into the bowl, causing an encore flush to occur. Fortunately, the only adverse consequence is wasted water. Some low-flow toilets require two flushes to get the job done anyway. In this case, the backup flush is on autopilot. If you wish to have this corrected, refer the matter to a licensed plumber.

---

64. ☐ **Toilet runs continuously.** If the tank flapper remains in the up position after the toilet is flushed, the tank will not refill, and water will continue running until the flush handle is jiggled. The cause may be faulty hardware or poor adjustment.

65. ☐ **Flush valve leaks in tank.** A leaking flush valve is only observable by lifting the tank lid when the fixture is flushing. Replacement of the valve is usually necessary.

66. ☐ **Flapper leaks in tank.** The flapper is the stopper at the base of the tank whose purpose is to release the tank water into the bowl when the toilet is flushed. If the flapper does not form a tight seal against the water

Tank is visibly cracked.

outlet, continuous seepage occurs, causing the water level in the tank to recede. To compensate, the tank valve refills the tank every few minutes. The result is a high monthly water bill.

67. ☐ Rotted wood flooring. Decay of the subfloor usually results from a moisture condition at the base of the toilet, indicating a leaking wax seal, as noted above. This should be reviewed and repaired by a licensed pest control operator because of fungus infection to the wood framing and sheathing.

Time to empty the cup or fix the leak.

68. ☐ Floor vinyl is discolored or loose. Discolored vinyl at the base of a toilet is evidence of leaking at the wax seal, as noted above.

69. ☐ Cracks in the toilet fixture. When cracks are apparent in the bowl, base, or tank, replacement of the toilet is recommended. When the lid is damaged, finding one that fits the tank is nearly impossible, unless the toilet is relatively new.

70. ☐ Other miscellaneous toilet defects. We could continue listing the potential defects involving the mechanical components and functional aspects of toilet fixtures, but having considered more than a dozen such conditions, it's time to get our minds out of the toilet.

Base of bowl is visibly cracked.

Elbow room is inadequate. Center of toilet must be at least 15 inches from wall.

Sinks, Tubs, and Showers

As with the plumbing conditions already reviewed, there is a lengthy list of faulty conditions involving sinks, tubs, showers, and appurtenant fixtures. These range from cosmetic imperfections to serious plumbing defects. Among the most common are the following:

71. ☐ **Stains and discoloration.** Stains are cosmetic defects that can range in severity from inadequate cleaning to permanent etching of porcelain surfaces. Such conditions are typically listed in an inspection report for disclosure purposes only.

72. ☐ **Cracked or chipped sinks.** Chipped sink surfaces are generally regarded as wear-and-tear disclosures in an inspection report. However, when sinks are cracked, replacement is often recommended.

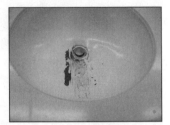

Sink finish is chipped and metal base is corroded. Underside of fixture is depicted in the illustration at right.

Severe rust damage is apparent under sink. Fixture needs replacement.

73. ☐ **Corrosion on underside of sink.** With cast-iron sinks, corrosion of the undersurface is generally not a matter for concern. With sheet metal sinks, rust damage is common and may warrant replacement of the fixture.

74. ☐ **Corrosion around drain openings.** Corrosion often occurs at drain openings and is usually regarded as a cosmetic defect.

75. ☐ **Sink or cabinet not securely attached.** Sinks and cabinets that are not professionally installed are sometimes set in place without being fastened. Movement can result in leakage at the plumbing connections. Therefore, repair is recommended.

Cracks commonly develop in cultured marble sinks.

76. ☐ **Low water volume.** Restricted or reduced water flow at faucets may indicate minor problems, such as debris in the faucet screens, or major defects, such as deteriorated water piping. If cleaning the screens is not effective, evaluation by a licensed plumber is recommended.

77. ☐ **Leaking at faucet handles.** Faulty seals can cause leaking at faucet handles. This is usually a minor plumbing defect.

78. ☐ **Leaking at faucet base.** When leaking occurs at the faucet base, the cause may be a leaking seal or a deteriorated faucet. Evaluation and repair or replacement by a licensed plumber is recommended.

79. ☐ **Hot and cold reversed.** The plumbing code requires hot water on the left side of a faucet and cold on the right. This is to prevent accidental scalding, since people are accustomed to the conventional positioning of hot and cold water.

80. ☐ **Dripping at spout.** When faucets drip, the common cause is a defective washer, although sometimes the valve seats may also be defective.

Tub faucet hardware is missing.

81. ☐ **Problems with supply valves.** Water supply valves (also known as angle stops) are located below sinks and are sometimes found to be corroded or leaking. Angle stops often become stuck due to lack of use. Home inspectors rarely test them because they often begin to leak when the handles are turned.

82. ☐ **Faulty drains.** Drains should be checked for leakage and a reasonable rate of water flow.

83. ☐ **Substandard drains.** There are numerous noncomplying ways of installing sink, tub, and shower drains, including S-traps, lack of a trap, lack of a vent, lack of proper slope, lack of a cleanout, and so on.

84. ☐ **Signs of past leakage.** Residual water stains and moderate water damage are signs of past leakage. Home inspectors typically point out these conditions for disclosure purposes only.

Rapid runaway drain leak below bathroom sink.

85. ☐ **Corroded fixtures.** Corrosion on plumbing fixtures can range from moderate cosmetic defects to severely damaged hardware in need of replacement.

86. ☐ **Moisture damage.** Moisture damage at plumbing fixtures can involve cabinets, walls, floors, and ceilings. Damage may

Leakage is likely to occur sooner or later at this creatively original tub-shower conversion.

involve routine cosmetic repair or evaluation and repair by a licensed pest control operator.

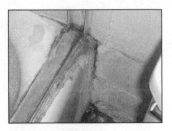

Leaking at corner of tub enclosure has caused severe moisture damage to wall and floor.

Stains on floor indicate leaking shower enclosure or pan. Water testing is needed.

87. ☐ **Leaking shower enclosures.** Shower enclosures often leak at the seams, the base, or the door seal, and such leakage can cause damage to walls or flooring. Therefore, preventive maintenance is recommended.

88. ☐ **Defective shower enclosures.** Shower enclosure defects can range from those that leak to those that are damaged, improperly built, or unsafe.

Damaged shower door unit needs replacement with tempered safety glass door and enclosure.

A leaking shower pan can thoroughly rot the underlying floor structure.

89. ☐ **Leaking shower pan.** Shower pans are generally checked by pest control operators, rather than by home inspectors, because leakage can result in fungus infection of the adjacent and underlying wood members. Testing is done by blocking the drain and filling the pan with water. Repair of a leaking pan entails reconstruction of the shower stall floor.

ASK THE INSPECTOR

Keeping Whirlpool Bathtubs Safe

Dear Barry,

Please help me resolve a debate I'm having with a local home inspector. I have a small business installing bathtub whirlpool systems. For added safety, I use plastic pipe to prevent electrical connections between the tub and pump equipment. On several occasions, this inspector has faulted my installations for lack of ground fault protection. I've explained that plastic piping cannot conduct electricity from the pump to the tub, but he insists that GFCI protection is required. How can I convince him that these systems are safe without adding a GFCI outlet?

Jim

Dear Jim,

Sorry to let you down, but the gold medal goes to the home inspector. Ground fault circuit interrupters (GFCI) are designed to prevent injury or death from electric shock by shutting off the power in the event that current is diverted from the circuit. Common sense demands this type of protection where bathtubs are connected to electrical equipment.

The use of plastic pipe to prevent electrical contact between a tub and pump seems practical at first glance, but you've overlooked a crucial consideration: the water itself can conduct electricity, unless your customers are bathing in distilled water. Dissolved minerals render the water highly conductive, just as the liquid in your car's battery. If the pump should ever develop a leak, 120 volts could light up the water with electrifying consequences to the unsuspecting bather.

The logical and practical solution is to install a simple GFCI outlet in the power line to the pump. The additional cost for materials is approximately $10. By including this added protection for your customers, you will not only resolve your conflict with the home inspector, but you will also maintain legal compliance with the National Electrical Code.

---

90. ☐ **Lack of safety glass.** Safety glass is required at shower enclosures and at most windows adjacent to bathtubs and showers, although older homes may predate some of these requirements. Upgrades at old showers are recommended but are usually not mandatory.

91. ☐ **Room ventilation.** Bathrooms must be vented to the exterior of the building by means of an openable window or an exhaust fan. Related defects include unopenable windows, fans that are inoperative, fans that vent into an attic, fans that are unusually noisy, lack of a window or fan, and so on. Unvented bathrooms are prone to moisture damage and mold as a result of condensation.

Mold infection is apparent in this shower. Due to recent concerns regarding hazardous varieties of mold, professional testing is often recommended by home inspectors.

A towel bar installed above an electric wall heater can cause a fire.

92. ☐ **Bathroom heaters.** Bathroom heaters should be checked for condition and operability. However, it is generally not a requirement that bathrooms be heated.

Kitchen Plumbing

Evaluation of kitchen plumbing involves many of the conditions noted in the bathroom section above, plus many others. Among these are the following:

93. ☐ **Faulty conditions at the kitchen sink area include:**
- Sinks that are discolored, corroded, chipped, cracked, or loose
- Low water volume
- Leaking faucet handles
- Leaking faucet base
- Faulty hand sprayer
- Hot and cold reversed
- Dripping at spout
- Problems with supply valves
- Faulty drains
- Substandard drains
- Signs of past leakage
- Corroded fixtures
- Moisture damage

Drain leakage and moisture damage are apparent below kitchen sink. Reverse osmosis tank is sinking into decayed cabinet floor.

For explanatory comments pertaining to the foregoing list, see the bathroom plumbing section above.

94. ☐ **Loud or vibrating garbage disposal.** Noise and vibration generally indicate that a disposal is old, worn out, and in need of replacement.

95. ☐ **Faulty garbage disposal wiring.** Common electrical defects include lack of an outlet for the power cord, wiring without a conduit, exposed splices, lack of grounding, a switch connected to the neutral wire, and so on.

Disposal is hard-wired, with no outlet to enable disconnection of power supply.

Excessive corrosion at base of old disposal.

96. ☐ **Excessive corrosion.** Rust and corrosion indicate that the disposal is old and may have limited remaining life.

97. ☐ **Condition of splash guard.** The flexible rubber covering at the disposal opening prevents particles from being ejected when the unit is in use. Damaged or missing splash guards should be replaced to prevent possible eye injuries.

Splash guard needs replacement.

98. ☐ **Disposal unit inoperative.** When old disposals become jammed or are otherwise inoperative, the time for replacement has usually arrived.

99. ☐ **Hazardous switch location.** A disposal switch should not be installed on the cabinet face, where the fixture can be activated when someone leans against the cabinet. The reason is simple: Suppose that you reach into the disposal to retrieve a bottle cap or sponge. You lean against the cabinet; the switch is moved; good-bye fingers.

Garbage disposal switch can be inadvertently turned on by leaning against the cabinet.

100. ☐ **Dishwasher without an airgap.** A dishwasher airgap is the small chrome cylinder on the rear rim of your sink. It's the thing that gurgles when your dishwasher is draining. The purpose of the airgap is to prevent a sewage backup from contaminating the interior of the dishwasher. Some plumbing codes require airgaps, but others do not. Installing an airgap is a good idea, regardless of whether it is mandated.

Someone asked why the home inspector didn't test the dishwasher (fixture used as a pantry).

Internal rust damage is typical of an aging dishwasher.

101. ☐ **Dishwasher makes unusual noise.** Noisiness in a dishwasher may indicate a number of potential problems. The solutions, as with most dishwasher problems, is to call a qualified appliance technician.

102. ☐ **Miscellaneous dishwasher defects.** Various dishwasher defects that warrant attention by a qualified appliance technician include rust damage, leakage, faulty soap dispenser, faulty door seal, lack of proper attachment to the cabinet, defective door hardware, and so on.

Water draining from dishwasher airgap indicates blockage in line.

Laundry Plumbing

Common laundry defects include the following:

103. ☐ **Defective sink plumbing.** These conditions are the same as noted in the preceding sections and include problems involving
faucets, drains, and sinks.

104. ☐ **Faulty gas connections.** Gas piping is
often provided for a clothes dryer. Violations
include lack of a gas shutoff valve, joining
flex connectors in series, unsecured gas piping, unapproved gas pipe materials, and
others.

*Homeowner connected laundry
sink to sump pump because basement is located below sewer lines.*

105. ☐ **Substandard washer drain.** Faulty washer drain conditions include,
among others, lack of a trap, undersized piping, draining to the yard area,
and lack of proper height for the standpipe.

*Air inlet vents, such as this one, are
currently approved for mobile
homes and may soon be permitted
in conventional dwellings.*

*Dryer exhaust vents into attic,
causing lint build-up and excessive
moisture.*

106. ☐ **Substandard dryer vent.** Faulty dryer vent conditions include venting
exhaust into the building, venting exhaust below the building or into the
attic, using unapproved duct material, using screws to secure duct fittings,
installing a dryer vent through a furnace plenum, exceeding 14 feet in the
total run of the duct, and so on.

107. ☐ **Washer connections.** Water supply connections for washing machines
are often prone to leakage and may be corroded or improperly installed.

HEATING CHECKLIST

The two primary concerns when inspecting a heating system are safety and operability, in that order. With numerous types of heating systems commonly in use, considerable knowledge and experience are necessary to qualify an inspector in this aspect of property evaluation, and homebuyers should beware of attempting this type of inspection on their own.

Fuel-Burning Forced-Air Heat

The most common form of residential heating in North American homes is the warm air system, typically fueled with natural gas, but also fueled with propane, oil, or other combustion materials where natural gas is not available. These systems consist of a furnace in which air is heated and then circulated, by way of metal, plastic, or fiberglass ducts, to various rooms throughout the building. Many functional and safety concerns are incorporated into inspections of these systems. Among the countless considerations for home inspectors when inspecting forced-air heating systems are the following:

1. ☐ **Evidence of overdue servicing.** Warm air heating systems should be serviced annually so that developing problems can be foreseen and circumvented. Rust flakes in the burner chambers and dust buildup within the main air unit indicate deferred maintenance. Failure to conduct periodic review of a furnace can have life-threatening consequences if developing safety problems go undiscovered.

Dust buildup in return air system indicates that fixture is long overdue for professional servicing.

2. ☐ **Inadequate combustion air supply.** Essential to safe gas combustion is having an adequate supply of air. Furnaces installed in enclosed spaces, such as closets, must have air openings that comply with specific code requirements.

3. ☐ **Unusual noise or vibration.** Noisy or vibrating furnaces usually indicate problems with the blower motor or its bearings.

4. ☐ **Response to controls.** Furnaces should be checked for normal response to control settings on the thermostat.

5. ☐ **Intermittent performance.** Burners and blowers may cycle on and off repeatedly, indicating faulty adjustment of sensing equipment or defective system components.

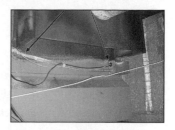

6. ☐ **Fire safety clearances.** Furnaces are required to have specified clearances from adjacent walls and other nearby building components to prevent the furnace equipment and other materials from becoming overheated.

Moisture at draft diverter is damaging electrical hardware.

7. ☐ **Damaged heat exchanger.** The heat exchanger is the combustion chamber where fuel is burned in a furnace. Cracks or holes in a heat exchanger can cause carbon monoxide to mix with the warm air that is circulated into the home. This is the most significant hazard that can occur with a furnace.

Hot flue pipe touches flammable sheathing on air duct.

Heat exchanger is damaged. Furnace needs replacement.

8. ☐ **Flame pattern and color.** A flame that is yellow or orange, instead of blue, or a flame whose shape is irregular or tends to fluctuate, is an indication of major safety problems that could be life threatening and could necessitate replacement of the furnace. When the blower turns on, changes in the flame characteristics may indicate a damaged heat exchanger.

ASK THE INSPECTOR

Gas Company Provides Protection for Buyers

Dear Barry,

We just purchased a 20-year-old home and had it checked out by a home inspector. According to the inspection report, the wall heater was in good working order, but the gas company has just declared it to be unsafe. According to the gas man, there is a hole in the heat exchanger, and the entire furnace needs to be replaced. Shouldn't this condition have been found by the home inspector?

Lonnie

Dear Lonnie,

Experienced home inspectors are often able to detect cracks or holes in heat exchangers, but in many cases the damage is not visually discernable and requires expertise that exceeds the scope of a general visual inspection. At times, it is even necessary to dismantle the fixture. In some cases, however, symptoms such as unusual flame patterns or back-drafting exhaust can alert a home inspector to a faulty heat exchanger without actually seeing the hole or crack. Unfortunately, not all home inspectors are acquainted with such observations.

A damaged heat exchanger is a very serious defect because it enables combustion gases, such as carbon monoxide, to enter the dwelling. Detection, therefore, is vitally important. For this reason, many home inspectors have come to recognize the value of gas company inspections in conjunction with their own evaluations.

For anyone purchasing a home, it is extremely prudent to have the gas company perform a safety check of all gas-burning fixtures prior to closing the sale. This is a free service that the gas company routinely provides upon request. In addition to adjusting the burners on stoves, water heaters, and furnaces, they check for serious safety problems. When defects or hazardous conditions exist, the gas company can help to discover them before you take possession of the property.

---

9. ☐ **Rust flakes at burner.** Corrosion in the burner chamber may indicate the development of cracks or holes in the heat exchanger. Further evaluation is warranted.

10. ☐ **Charring or soot.** Blackened surfaces or soot particles in or around the burners or the exhaust vent indicate combustion problems that may be hazardous. Further evaluation is warranted because there are several potential causes for these symptoms.

Severe rusting in heat exchanger warrants immediate evaluation.

Charred metal surface indicates faulty combustion or venting at second burner. Furnace should not be used in this condition.

11. ☐ **Flame rollout.** When the flames protrude from the burner access opening, there are problems with the combustion and/or the exhaust venting. This condition is hazardous and warrants further evaluation.

12. ☐ **Flue too close to combustibles.** Exhaust piping for a furnace must be installed with required clearances to combustible materials. Violations are often found in attics.

Hot flue pipe makes contact with wood and electrical wires.

Flue terminates near an openable window. Exhaust can vent into dwelling.

13. ☐ **Flue termination at roof.** A flue pipe must terminate at minimum required distances from roof surfaces and from openings such as doors or windows. These requirements are intended for fire safety and to prevent exhaust from venting into a building.

14. ☐ **Condition of flue cap.** A flue pipe should terminate with an approved type of cap to prevent rain leakage and exhaust backup due to wind.

Top of flue cap has rusted through.

Flue pipe must have continuous upward slope for proper exhaust venting.

15. ☐ **Rise of flue pipe.** A flue pipe, when installed horizontally, should have the required degree of upward slope to promote the proper venting of exhaust. Where the flue system is not equipped with an induction fan, there are also requirements that regulate the relative lengths of the horizontal and vertical portions of the flue pipe.

16. ☐ **Damage or corrosion.** Flue pipes should be checked for damage that could enable exhaust gases to escape.

Flue pipe is severely rusted.

17. ☐ **Combustion air supply.** A furnace must have a continuous source of oxygen to promote complete combustion of the fuel. There are many requirements in this regard, including specifications for the size and location of air vents; prohibited sources of air (such as bedrooms); distances between combustion air sources and return air openings; dampers and screens on air openings; gaps or other openings between the furnace enclosure and the return air plenum; and many more.

18. ☐ **Fuel supply.** Fuel connections should be checked for leaks, for use of approved materials, for proper installation of a shutoff valve, and for installation of fuel piping in ways that comply with applicable safety requirements.

19. ☐ **Condition of air ducts.** Warm air ducts should be checked for secure attachment at the fittings (often a problem in attics and below buildings), for physical damage, for internal buildup of dust and debris, for lack of insulation, for insulation that may contain asbestos, for leaking air, and so on.

An extension pipe is needed so that flex connector can attach outside the furnace casing.

Ducts on ground can incur moisture intrusion and develop mold.

How to heat your attic in one easy step.

ASK THE INSPECTOR

Getting All Your Ducts in a Row

Dear Barry,

Allow me to take exception to your recent article advising the cleaning of forced-air heating ducts. I don't believe there is much evidence to support the benefits of duct cleaning. Although it probably won't hurt, it bears pointing out that the U.S. Environmental Protection Agency (EPA) does not recommend duct cleaning and has no evidence that it improves human health.

David

Dear David,

If you could view the interior surfaces of forced-air heating ducts, as seen by home inspectors and heating, ventilating, and air conditioning (HVAC) contractors, you would be appalled at the prospect of inhaling air that is discharged from some of these outlets. This is certainly not the case with all forced-air systems, but occupants in many homes are unknowingly breathing air that has been circulated over layers of visible filth.

In older homes, many forced-air heaters have been operated for years with dirty filters or no filters at all. The accumulated dust on the inner duct surfaces is often oily or moist and may contain mites or various species of molds or fungus. In newer homes, where airtight construction methods are employed for enhanced energy conservation, the growth of mold spores has become recognized as a significant indoor air quality hazard. In these cases, air ducts provide a common harbor and distribution mechanism for biological air contaminants. To discount these realities, simply because some government agency has failed to recognize them is to accord a higher level of trust and dependence upon bureaucratic institutions than such entities fairly warrant. Sooner or later, the EPA is likely to acknowledge the potential health hazards associated with dirty warm air ducts. But the problem will continue to exist, with or without that recognition.

20. ☐ **Air filters.** Common problems include filters that are dirty, missing, damaged, or not adequately secured.

21. ☐ **Insufficient airflow.** Lack of adequate airflow can indicate a dirty filter, blockage of the air distribution system, or poor design of the ducting. Further evaluation by a licensed HVAC contractor is usually warranted.

A dirty filter reduces heating efficiency and can damage the furnace due to overheating.

22. ☐ **Miscellaneous conditions.** Additional conditions, too numerous to list, that involve the safety and operability of furnaces, are also considered in the course of a home inspection.

Other Types of Gas Heaters

Other common types of gas heating systems include wall furnaces, floor furnaces, and suspended space heaters. Many of the considerations noted in the forced-air section above also apply to wall, floor,

A work platform and light fixture are required at this attic furnace. Also, the owners manual is combustible and should not be in contact with the unit.

and space heaters. These include conditions pertaining to fire safety clearances, physical damage, corrosion, the condition and function of burners, charring and soot, gas connections, gas leaks, exhaust venting, combustion air supply, thermostats, and so on.

Piping for this hot water heating system consists of copper and steel in direct contact. This generates electrolysis that promotes corrosion.

Soot on furnace and wall indicates back-drafting of exhaust into home. The inspector who discovered this may have saved the happy family shown in the photographs.

Hot Water Heating Systems

In some areas of the country, a common heat medium is hot water or steam circulated through room radiators, through radiant piping in a concrete slab floor, or through a heat exchanger in a forced-air system. Fuels for such systems include natural gas, propane, oil, coal, wood, and electricity. The components that comprise these systems pose major operational and safety considerations for an inspector, particularly because of the high internal pressures to which steam heating systems are subjected. Many of these concerns are the same as those with other fuel-burning systems, but with further issues to be considered. Additional items typically inspected include:

23. ☐ **Evidence of leakage.** Boilers and fittings are subject to water or steam leakage due to high internal operating pressures.

24. ☐ **Damage and corrosion.** Boilers and fittings should be checked for damage or corrosion that might result in leakage or impaired function.

25. ☐ **Pressure and temperature.** The safe performance of a boiler system depends upon maintaining specified pressure levels and operating temperatures.

26. ☐ **Circulating systems.** The heat distribution portion of the system should be checked for signs of damage or corrosion and for proper installation. With older systems, major deterioration may require replacement of all or part of the system.

Heat distribution in steam systems is often done with radiators such as this one.

ASK THE INSPECTOR

Buyers Concerned about Steam Heat Pipes

Dear Barry,

We are purchasing a 1910, three-story home. Our home inspector said the house was previously heated by steam but has been converted to hot water heating. The problem, he says, is that the pipes were not changed. He explained that pipes intended for steam are not the same diameter as those installed for hot water and that this affects the efficiency of the system. The boiler is functional but will soon *need replacement. When we replace it, should we convert back to steam heat or replace the piping to accommodate hot water heating?*

Richelle

Dear Richelle,

Your home inspector's opinion and recommendation were accurate. The design and layout of steam pipes differ significantly from hot water heating systems, owing to the dissimilar characteristics of these two heat media. Inappropriate piping can reduce the efficiency and effectiveness of these systems.

Steam pipes must slope upward at the supply lines to prevent water in the system from restricting the flow of steam. Also, these pipes should decrease in diameter as they proceed away from the boiler. The return pipes must be smaller in diameter than the supply pipes, as they carry water instead of steam. In addition, steam pipes need insulation on the supply side only; the return pipes should be uninsulated in order to promote condensation.

With hot water heating systems, the diameter of the piping remains constant, the slope is irrelevant, and all lines are insulated to prevent heat loss. Therefore, the house you are buying should have been repiped when the current system was installed. If you stay with hot water heating, the costs to complete the system conversion could be quite high. The piping would require replacement, and this could entail serious demolition and repairs to the interior walls and other portions of the home. What's more, replacement of the radiators, valves, and vents would be necessary if this has not already been done.

If most of the original system was left intact, restoration of steam heating would be advisable. For a specific comparison of costs to restore steam heat or complete the conversion to a hot water system, consult a licensed heating contractor in your area.

---

27. ☐ **Fuel connections.** Fuel supply considerations for hot water and steam heating systems are the same as listed in item 18 above.

28. ☐ **Exhaust venting.** Concerns pertaining to combustion exhaust are the same as listed in items 11–16 above.

29. ☐ **Combustion air.** Combustion air requirements for hot water and steam heating systems are the same as listed in item 17 above.

30. ☐ **Miscellaneous.** Boiler heating systems involve numerous additional technical complexities requiring consideration by a professional inspector.

Electric Heating

Electric heat was commonly installed in homes built from the mid-1950s through the early 1970s and continues as the standard in areas of the country where combustion fuels are not readily available. In the heyday of electrical heating, the cost of electricity was nominal, and few foresaw the major escalation in power costs that were just ahead. Electric heat was promoted on the basis of being clean, safe, and cheap. In homes with these systems, it is still clean and relatively safe, but maintaining warmth in these dwellings is usually far from cheap.

Conditions that warrant inspection are as follows:

31. ☐ **Radiant ceiling heat.** Radiant ceilings are heated by a grid of wires contained within the drywall. These become warm when operated, producing clean, quiet heat. But heat, as everyone knows, tends to rise, making a ceiling system very inefficient. However, radiant ceiling heat is generally free of functional defects so long as no one drills holes in the ceiling. When homeowners hang a plant or swag lamp, a wire can be severed, rendering the system inoperative.

32. ☐ **Electric wall heaters.** An electric wall heater typically consists of heat coils, with or without a blower. These should be checked for operability and physical damage. It is also important to keep these fixtures clear of combustible materials such as curtains and furniture. In bathrooms, towel bars should never be installed above electric wall heaters.

33. ☐ **Electric baseboard heaters.** Baseboard heaters provide radiant-type heating. Inspection of these devices is also limited to determining operability and assessing for physical damage. As with electric wall heaters, safe clearance to combustible materials must be maintained.

34. ☐ **Electric forced-air systems.** Electric warm air systems come in various types, some providing heat only, whereas others are integrated with air conditioning systems. Evaluation of the inner workings of the heat-producing unit itself is clearly beyond the range of the average homebuyer. In fact, even home inspectors perform limited evaluations of such equipment, reporting mainly on issues of operability, physical condition, and compliance with regard to electrical connections. Inspections of these systems also

Exterior vent in return air duct reduces efficiency of system by drawing cold outside air into the furnace.

include air ducts, air registers, thermostats, filters, and whatever portions of such systems are accessible without dismantling the components.

The foregoing does not include all types of heating systems, nor does it cover alternative types of heating, such as active solar, passive solar, or geothermal heating. The purpose of this section, rather, has been to present conditions commonly inspected in the most prevalent types of heating systems in American homes.

COOLING SYSTEMS CHECKLIST

Cooling systems consist primarily of air conditioners and evaporative coolers. Air conditioners are basically refrigeration systems that produce cold air. Evaporative coolers work on the principle that evaporation of water uses up heat; when air is drawn through a wet fabric (known as a cooler pad), evaporation reduces the temperature of the air.

Air Conditioners

Central air conditioners are typically integral components of forced-air heating systems. Therefore, many aspects of central air conditioning (AC) systems, such as air ducts, filters, and electrical connections, are included in the heating portion of the inspection. Other pertinent conditions include the following:

1. ☐ **Insufficient cooling.** When the system has been operating for several minutes, the outflow at the air registers should be at least 20 degrees cooler than the ambient room temperature. Some inspectors determine this in a general way by placing a hand over each register, while others use sophisticated test equipment to obtain an accurate reading. When the air is not sufficiently cooled, the most common cause is lack of refrigerant. Such problems warrant attention by a licensed HVAC contractor.

Major corrosion at base of A/C compressor unit.

2. ☐ **Unit is noisy.** When the A/C unit vibrates or is noisy, motor bearings or other mechanical components may need repair or replacement. Noisiness or vibration may also indicate that the unit is old and worn out.

3. ☐ Insufficient airflow. Lack of adequate airflow can indicate a dirty filter, blockage of the air distribution system, or poor design of the ducting. Further evaluation by a licensed HVAC contractor is usually warranted.

Major corrosion at base of wall mount A/C unit.

Condensate pipe drains onto wall and window.

4. ☐ Faulty condensate lines. A/C systems produce condensate from ambient air moisture. This must be piped to the exterior of the building to prevent moisture damage. Common defects, among others, include lack of primary condensate piping, lack of secondary condensate piping, lack of a trap or vent, connection of the condensate pipe to a plumbing waste line, draining condensate onto the roof, and line leakage.

Condensate drain is connected to a waste vent. This can allow sewer gases into the A/C system.

Gaps where pipes enter air plenum allow conditioned air to escape from the system.

5. ☐ Lack of electrical shutoff. An electrical disconnect switch is required near an A/C unit to protect contractors and technicians from electrical shock when systems are being serviced.

6. ☐ **Miscellaneous conditions.** Air conditioners are complex systems for which a detailed evaluation requires the services of a licensed HVAC contractor. Home inspectors typically provide a limited observational review of general condition and operability. Other miscellaneous considerations include physical damage to components, unstable placement of the A/C unit, substandard electrical wiring, lack of insulation on refrigerant lines, and so on.

Unprotected refrigerant lines are buried in ground and embedded in pavement.

Evaporative Coolers

Commonly known as "swamp coolers," these fixtures are typically mounted on rooftops or windows and provide cool air at a specific location, rather than being centrally distributed through a system of air ducts. As noted above, cooling of the air is produced by the evaporation of water. Conditions typically inspected include the following:

Major rust damage at evaporative cooler.

7. ☐ **Water leakage.** Leaking can occur at the base of the evaporative unit or at water lines because of loose or corroded connections, rust damage at the water basin, a faulty fill valve, or various other conditions.

8. ☐ **Damage due to corrosion.** Rust and corrosion are common with older units, as they were generally constructed of ferrous metals. Rust damage usually indicates that the unit is ready for replacement. Newer units are typically made of plastic and, therefore, are not prone to corrosion.

9. ☐ **Deteriorated cooler pads.** Evaporative cooler pads can eventually disintegrate and often become congested with residual minerals. Annual reinspection of these pads should be done as part of normal home maintenance.

10. ☐ **Unit is noisy.** If the evaporative unit vibrates or is noisy, motor bearings or other mechanical components may need repair or replacement. Vibration and noisiness may also indicate that the unit is old and worn out.

11. ☐ **Water shutoff.** A water valve should be located at or near the unit to enable the system to be turned off and drained. The valve should be checked for corrosion, leakage, and operability.

12. ☐ **Miscellaneous.** Additional items to be inspected include the general condition of all visible components and the overall operability of the system.

BUILDING EXTERIOR CHECKLIST

The exterior surfaces of a building, including walls, trim, and eaves, are routinely inspected for evidence of damage, deterioration, and faulty construction. Conditions routinely inspected are as follows:

1. ☐ **Cracked or deteriorated stucco.** Most stucco defects are cosmetic in nature, including hairline cracks and crumbly surface finish on older buildings, particularly where stucco makes contact with the soil.

2. ☐ **Cracked or deteriorated siding.** Solid wood siding is subject to cracking and warping. Deterioration of plywood siding usually involves delamination of the veneer. Composite cellulose siding (Masonite-type material) is subject to moderate or excessive warping and decomposition. Problems with cellulose siding are usually moisture related and, in severe cases, are usually the result of faulty installation or defective manufacture.

Movement of garden wall has damaged stucco on building.   *Cellulose hardboard siding is badly warped due to moisture.*

3. ☐ **Weathered surfaces.** Weathering, including peeling paint or oxidized wood surfaces, is the result of deferred exterior maintenance. Repainting weathered surfaces does not restore the finish to the same quality as when repainting precedes weather damage.

4. ☐ **Damaged surfaces.** Exterior damage, aside from weathering and wear, includes such defects as holes in wall and trim surfaces, rotted wood, badly rusted hardware, and more.

Leaking dual pane window, as observed from exterior.

Dryrot or termite damage is apparent at base of support post.

5. ☐ **Faulty windows.** Exterior window defects include rotted wood, broken panes, deteriorated seals, cracked or missing sash putty, corroded hardware, missing or damaged screens, and more.

6. ☐ **Faulty doors.** Exterior door defects include rotted wood at the door, jamb, or trim; delamination of the door veneer; rust damage; defective latch hardware; and more.

Some occupants appreciate the advantages of a damaged door.

Post is not securely fastened, and hardware is damaged.

7. ☐ **Miscellaneous defects.** These include any type of damage to any exterior surfaces. The possibilities are endless.

YARD AREA CHECKLIST

1. ☐ **Fencing.** Fence repairs are part of normal property maintenance. Unless fences are relatively new, they are likely to have some deterioration, rotted wood, leaning or loose posts, cracked masonry, damaged hardware, gates in need of adjustments, and other problems.

Fence collapsed due to rotted posts.

Retaining wall is separating at non-reinforced corners.

2. ☐ **Retaining walls.** Repair or replacement of defective retaining walls can be costly and important, especially if the walls are high and if they support ground areas that are essential to the stability of a building. When retaining walls have major cracks or leaning, evaluation by a licensed structural engineer is warranted.

3. ☐ **Driveways.** Driveways typically have common hairline cracks. Larger cracks may warrant repair if they pose trip hazards. Surface water drainage should also be considered when inspecting a driveway, as faulty drainage can cause water intrusion into the garage.

Driveway is badly cracked, with some areas being trip hazards.

Patio is badly cracked, but effect is mainly cosmetic.

4. ☐ **Walkways and patios.** As with driveways, other paved surfaces typically have hairline cracks and should be inspected for larger defects that constitute trip hazards. Drainage is also a concern with walkways and patios. All pavement should provide drainage away from buildings.

5. ☐ **Porches and decks.** Wood porches and decks are highly prone to fungus infection, resulting in dryrot. Such conditions are typically reported by pest control operators, but home inspectors also disclose such damage when it is observed. Safety concerns with porches and decks involve railings and their compliance with applicable standards.

Severe wood decay is evident at hole in deck membrane.

ASK THE INSPECTOR

Earth to Wood Contact at Deck

Dear Barry,

The wood deck behind my house is in contact with the soil. The people who are buying my home insist that no wood should be touching the soil. I've explained that the deck can't affect the building because the walls are made of stucco. How can I get them to see that their concerns are unwarranted?

Kevin

Dear Kevin,

In all likelihood, the sale of your home will involve the services of a termite inspection company whose job will be to determine whether earth to wood contact at the deck is likely to affect the house. If the deck adjoins the building at stucco surfaces only, then resultant damage to the house is unlikely. However, be sure to consider whether the deck is attached to any of the wood trim. That would cast a different light on the matter.

---

6. ☐ **Stairways.** Numerous safety standards apply to the layout of stairs and railings. Also, wood staircases are prone to fungus damage, as are decks and porches.

7. ☐ **Irrigation system.** Some home inspectors test landscape irrigation systems, and others do not. In either case, it is advisable to have the seller fully demonstrate the operation of the system before the sale is closed.

8. ☐ **Landscaping.** The health and condition of plants are not within the scope of a home inspection. However, home inspectors typically report situations where plants are adversely affecting buildings, such as vines growing

on walls, tree limbs touching the roof, tree limbs too close to the chimney top, or tree roots too close to the foundation.

Deck stairs need handrails, and short riser at top step is a trip hazard.

Sprinkler valve overflows at vacuum breaker.

GARAGE CHECKLIST

Some aspects of a garage inspection are redundant, relative to the dwelling inspection itself, especially where the garage is attached to the home. Overlapping considerations include the roof, exterior walls, windows, and trim. But there are also unique aspects of a garage that warrant particular considerations, with some involving vital safety issues. Conditions routinely inspected include the following:

1. ☐ **Physical condition.** Interior and exterior surfaces of a garage are inspected for damage, deterioration, faulty construction, substandard alterations, and more.

2. ☐ **Fire separation.** Wall and ceiling surfaces that separate a garage from a dwelling must comply with standards for a one-hour fire separation (wall construction theoretically designed to resist the spread of fire for one hour). This typically requires the use of ⅝-inch fire-rated drywall, with all joints

Someone asked why the home inspector did not fully inspect the garage.

taped, and all openings in compliance with firewall standards. A common violation is the addition of a folding ladder in the garage ceiling.

3. ☐ **Fire door.** The interior door from the garage to the dwelling is part of the firewall and must therefore be fire rated and self-closing.

Some building departments approve folding ladders in fire-resistant garage ceilings, but fire department officials unanimously oppose them unless there is a firewall in the attic.

Installing a pet access in a garage fire door is a firewall violation that can negate fire insurance coverage.

ASK THE INSPECTOR

Requirements for Garage Fire Door

Dear Barry,

    We want to replace the door that leads from our garage into our home and would like to use a six-panel oak door. What is the fire safety requirement for a door between a house and garage?

Cheryl

Dear Cheryl,

    Fire-resistive construction is required between a garage and a dwelling. The code specifies that this be a one-hour, fire-rated wall. Any door that is part of a garage firewall must be solid core or fire rated and must also be self-closing. If you plan to use an oak panel door, be sure that it has a fire-rating tag on one of its edges.

———————————

4. ☐ **Garage door.** Garage doors should be checked for operability and safety, damage and deterioration, rotted wood, faulty hardware, and more.

5. ☐ **Automatic door opener.** Door openers should be checked for operability, physical condition, quality of installation, and particularly for automatic safety reverse.

Notching of garage ceiling beam has negated its structural integrity.

6. ☐ **Miscellaneous.** Sundry garage conditions include electrical, plumbing, heating, and laundry installations, typically found in garages. These are addressed in various other portions of this chapter.

Garage door opener needs a nearby ceiling outlet, rather than an extension cord.

Laundry chute in garage violates firewall.

ROOFING CHECKLIST

Homebuyers often include roofing conditions among their primary considerations when purchasing a home. This is an appropriate concern because roof replacement can be very costly, and roof leakage can be disruptive to daily life and cause considerable damage to the interior. Recognizing the importance of identifying roof problems, home inspectors routinely consider the following conditions:

1. ☐ **Composition shingles.** Standard roof shingles are available in varying degrees of quality, rated from 15 years to 40 years of expected life. Materials should be checked for proper installation, degree of wear, physical damage, and places where leakage appears likely. Some building departments allow a maximum of three layers of composition shingles; in other localities, only two layers are permitted.

Shingles are long overdue for replacement.

ASK THE INSPECTOR

Code Compliance versus Common Sense

Dear Barry,

We were ready to close escrow on our home when the buyers' home inspector stirred up trouble over the roof repairs. The house is about 35 years old and has two *layers of shingles. According to the roofing contractor, the building code allows a third layer to be applied; but the home inspector says the roof structure is sagging and should not be loaded with the weight of additional shingles. Removing the old material will add about $500 to the cost of the job, and we view this as a needless expense. As far as I'm concerned, the roof is strong enough to support another layer of shingles. If a third layer would truly be detrimental, it wouldn't be allowed by code. Don't you agree?*

Jeremy

Dear Jeremy,

You're right, I don't agree.

Although multiple roof layers are allowed, code requirements are not intended to be followed blindly. When the code recommends a maximum of three roof layers, the implied assumption is that the roof structure is framed and reinforced in compliance with other pertinent building codes. If your roof is currently sagging under the weight of two shingle layers, it is reasonable to assume that there is a general lack of integrity in the rafter framing. The building code defines itself as a "minimum standard." Therefore, codes should be applied to each situation in the light of common sense.

My advice is to embrace the uncomfortable truth and simply remove the old shingles, as the home inspector advised. This may cost a few hundred dollars more but will protect you from potential liability problems after you sell the home. And just to be on the safe side, have the roof framing checked to determine if reinforcement is needed.

---

2. ☐ **Wood shakes.** Wood shakes and wood shingles also come in varying degrees of quality, from 20 years to 40 years of duration. Shake roofs have lost popularity because fire insurance companies view them as high risk. These roofs should be inspected for proper installation, physical damage, and apparent wear. Nearly all shake roofs are in need of maintenance repairs.

Time to replace the old shake roof, whether or not it leaks.

ASK THE INSPECTOR

What's Up with Curling Shakes?

Dear Barry,

My home has a cedar shake roof. Why do some of these shakes curl up, while others next to them do not?

James

Dear James,

Shakes are manufactured by splitting the wood with the grain, which is why shakes come in irregular shapes, rather than being uniformly matched, as are shingles. Because of these irregularities in thickness and variations in grain patterns, not all shakes respond the same to weathering and to heat and moisture changes. Just as some wood beams twist and crack as they become dry, while others remain straight, likewise, some shakes alter their shapes in response to environmental changes, whereas others do not.

As your roof becomes older, replacement of some shakes will become necessary every few years, not only because of curling, but because some will split or wear through, exposing the tar paper underlayment and eventually causing leaks. Therefore, it is recommended that you have your roof evaluated and tuned up every three to five years.

---

3. ☐ **Low-slope roofing.** The number one problem with low-slope roofing is that it is often flat, lacking adequate pitch for water runoff; and the resultant ponding on flat roof surfaces increases the likelihood of leakage. Most low-slope roofs are covered with asphalt composition roofing paper that was installed with hot tar, but there are better alternative materials. These roofs should be checked for proper installation, damage, patching, signs of leakage, weathering, and wear.

It's time to stop patching and start replacing.

4. ☐ **Tile roofing.** Tile roofing is permanent if left alone but is subject to breakage underfoot. Therefore, tile roofs are often inspected from atop a ladder or from the ground with the aid of binoculars. Common defects include cracked or broken tiles, loose tiles, lack of mortar at specified locations, and tiles that are improperly installed.

Unsecured tiles are gradually sliding down.

5. ☐ **Metal roofing.** Sheet metal roofing, more commonly used on commercial buildings, is slowly gaining acceptance for use on residential roofs. This increasing popularity is due to its longevity, resilience, lack of required maintenance, and roof accessibility. Possible defects include improper installation, loose fasteners, lifted edges, and physical damage.

6. ☐ **Flashing.** The sheet metal fittings at roof edges, pipes, skylights, chimneys, vents, and the like are known as flashing. Proper placement of flashing reduces the likelihood of leakage and faulty roof drainage at these locations. Common defects include faulty installation, rust damage, lack of adequate sealant, or lack of flashing.

Framing beneath metal roofing needs repair or reinforcement to eliminate deflection (sagging).

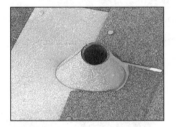

Flashing is improperly installed: pipe is too short, and flashing is penetrated with exposed nails.

7. ☐ **Skylights.** Roof windows, known as skylights, are highly prone to leakage unless properly installed and thoroughly flashed and sealed. Water stains on ceilings indicate past leakage. When these are found, water testing is recommended, along with review by a licensed roofing contractor.

Poorly installed skylight is guaranteed to leak, sooner or later.

8. ☐ **Drains.** Improved roof drainage is promoted by gutters on sloped roofs and scupper drains on flat roofs with parapet walls. These are generally inspected for proper installation and layout, physical damage, rust damage, looseness, signs of leakage, and conduction of downspouts away from the foundations.

Repeated patching at scupper drain indicates a history of leakage.

Attic framing member is damaged. Break occurred at large knot in wood.

9. ☐ **Attic framing.** The framing structure in an attic supports the weight of the roofing. Therefore, it is inspected for quality of construction, sagging wood members, physical damage, damage due to infestation, and more.

10. ☐ **Attic insulation.** Inspectors generally report on the type and amount of insulation in the attic. The effectiveness of the insulation is determined by its average total thickness.

11. ☐ **Attic ventilation.** Attics are vented to prevent overheating in the summer and moisture condensation in the winter. In most attics, ventilation is minimal because building standards that govern ventilation are marginally adequate.

Home inspectors would call this roof repair Mickey Mouse; I call it Goofy.

WOOD-BURNING FIXTURES CHECKLIST

Professional firefighters unanimously agree that defective fireplaces, along with faulty electrical conditions, rank among the primary causes of house fires. Therefore, inspection of fireplaces and wood-burning stoves is a major focus of any thorough property inspection. Among the conditions routinely evaluated are the following:

1. ☐ **Masonry firebox.** The firebox of a masonry fireplace is prone to various forms of deterioration, usually resulting from recurrent heat exposure and years of water intrusion at the chimney top. Common defects include cracked or loose bricks and soft or missing brick mortar.

Fire bricks and mortar are cracked and deteriorated.

ASK THE INSPECTOR

Chimney Cap Can Prevent Fireplace Damage

Dear Barry,

   The home I'm buying is only 12 years old, and already there is a major problem inside the fireplace. According to my home inspector, the mortar is crumbling and the firebricks are loose. I could understand this with a much older home. What could be the problem?

                                                                    Joel

Dear Joel,

   The inner linings of chimneys generally develop a coating of creosote; the substance that is removed when we hire a chimney sweep. When rainwater mixes with creosote, a mild acid is formed. This solution gradually seeps into the masonry lining, neutralizing the alkaline bond in the mortar. The result is that the mortar begins to weaken and disintegrate.

   The breakdown of fireplace mortar is common and can usually be prevented by installing a chimney cap. In many areas, caps are not required on masonry chimneys, but they should be. Have an approved cap installed on your chimney, and have the firebox repaired by a licensed masonry contractor.

---

2. ☐ **Manufactured firebox.** The firebox liner in a manufactured fireplace consists of ceramic plates that are fragile and prone to damage. A damaged refractory plate can cause overheating of the sheet metal casing that constitutes the outer shell of the fireplace.

Refractory plate is cracked in firebox.

3. ☐ **Masonry chimney.** The chimney of a masonry fireplace is prone to stress cracks and deteriorated mortar. Older masonry chimneys are typically unlined and are therefore regarded as unsafe for current use. Old masonry chimneys often show signs of settlement and may be visibly separated from the building.

Chimney is severely cracked. Fireplace should not be used.

Open chase top renders entire fireplace installation suspect. Further evaluation is warranted.

4. ☐ **Metal chimney.** Manufactured fireplaces and wood stoves typically have metal chimneys. These should be checked for proper installation, physical condition, and other conditions noted below.

5. ☐ **Height of chimney.** A chimney top must be at least two feet higher than any portion of the building within a radius of ten feet. This is the standard chimney height requirement.

Chimney is too short relative to nearby roof.

Chimney is too close to shrubbery.

6. ☐ **Clearance to chimney.** All chimneys are subject to clearance requirements to prevent heat exposure to adjacent combustible materials. Some clearances are standard dimensions set forth by the building code, and others are specific to particular manufactured products.

7. ☐ **Clearance to firebox.** Combustible materials at the front of a fireplace, including flooring, the mantle, and wall paneling, must comply with minimum fire safety clearance requirements to avoid unsafe heat exposure.

8. ☐ **Wood stove clearance.** Wood-burning stoves and free-standing fireplaces are subject to clearance requirements to prevent heat exposure to adjacent combustible materials. With unlisted stoves, clearances are standard dimensions set forth by the building code. With listed stoves, clearance requirements are specific to particular products.

Firebox is definitely too close to combustible flooring.

Wood stove lacks required clearance to walls.

9. ☐ **Gas fixture.** Gas fixtures should be properly installed, in undamaged condition, and specifically rated for the fireplaces in which they are used.

10. ☐ **Condition of damper.** Chimney dampers should be functional and undamaged. In fireplaces with gas logs, dampers should be secured in the open position to prevent combustion exhaust from venting into the dwelling.

Gap needs sealant where gas pipe penetrates wall of firebox.

11. ☐ **Creosote in chimney.** Creosote is the black residue that accumulates on the inside surfaces of chimneys and is the combustible material that results in chimney fires. Removing creosote is one of the primary functions of chimney sweeps.

12. ☐ **Spark arrester.** Every chimney top must have a screen to restrain cinders and prevent roof or tree fires. These screens should have openings no larger than ½ inch. On metal chimneys, the spark arrester should be part of the chimney cap.

Chimney is ready for the man with the top hat and tails.

13. ☐ **Soot above firebox.** Soot on the mantle or wall surface above the fireplace indicates that not all the smoke from the fireplace is drafting up the

chimney. However, soot above the fireplace could also mean that someone once started a fire with the damper closed.

Mortar cap and spark arrestor are missing.

Soot marks on mantle indicate inadequate draw.

14. ☐ **Water intrusion.** Moisture damage often occurs in fireplaces because no cap is installed to prevent rain intrusion. In many areas, caps are required only on metal chimneys.

15. ☐ **Chimney shroud.** A chimney shroud is a canopy or enclosure at the top of a chimney chase, added for architecturally aesthetic reasons. Chimney shrouds are often ordered from sheet metal shops rather than from the fireplace manufacturer. In such cases, the manufacturer's warranty may be voided.

Water stains in firebox indicate rain leakage at chimney top.

16. ☐ **Miscellaneous.** The possible defects likely to be found in the realm of fireplaces and wood stoves is nearly endless. They include, among others, bird nests in chimneys, homemade wood stoves, "handy-dandy" chimney fabrication, and substandard gas fixtures.

Chimney is unlined and severely deteriorated. Fireplace should not be used.

Someone asked, "Why must a chimney be lined?" Here's the answer, as viewed from within the attic.

BUILDING INTERIOR CHECKLIST

Interior defects range widely from normal wear to cosmetic damage; from major wear to severe damage; from water stains revealing past leakage to water damage indicating current leakage; from door and window problems involving routine adjustments to those requiring major repairs; and from minor stress cracks to major structural ones. There is much to be considered when inspecting the interior of a home and many decisions to be made regarding the severity of each condition. With this understanding, the following conditions are routinely inspected:

1. ☐ **Walls and ceilings.** Defective walls and ceilings range from cosmetic to structural symptoms. These surfaces should be checked for defects and irregularities of all kinds, including holes, cracks, peeling, wear, substandard materials, faulty workmanship, water damage, and on and on. Where cracks are found, the inspector must determine whether structural evaluation is warranted. Where moisture is involved, likely water sources should be determined, and further investigation may be needed to ascertain the extent of the damage.

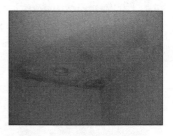

Before repairing ceiling, texture should be tested for asbestos content.

2. ☐ **Floors.** Floor defects also range from cosmetic to structural problems. Conditions inspected include damaged and worn floor coverings, moisture damage, sagging, sloping, substandard materials, faulty workmanship, and so on. When floors are not level, it should be determined whether structural problems may exist. Where moisture damage is found, further evaluation may also be needed.

Slab crack is visible through floor vinyl.

Subfloor is severely rotted at stall shower.

ASK THE INSPECTOR

Preventing Cracked Floor Tiles

Dear Barry,

We've got a new home under construction and have noticed cracks in the slab, right where the ceramic tile floor is to be installed. We're concerned that these cracks could affect the tiles. Is there anything we can do about this?

Michael

Dear Michael,

In most cases, common hairline stress cracks are not structural in nature, but they can still have an adverse effect on ceramic tile flooring. Slab cracks are generally not static fractures but tend to be subtly in motion, opening and closing with seasonal changes in temperature and ground moisture. To prevent resultant damage to tile flooring, your tile contractor should install a slip sheet on the slab prior to laying the tiles. This is a special fabric that is laminated to the slab surface, allowing slight movement at cracks, while preventing damage to the tiles.

---

3. ☐ **Doors.** Defects involving doors include minor damage, major damage, substandard workmanship, and symptoms of building settlement. Doors may be missing, poorly installed, stuck in the closed position, or unable to close. Hardware may be damaged, missing, inoperative, or not appropriate to the situation. Glass may be untempered; exterior doors may be rated for inside use only, and on and on.

Tempered glass is broken at sliding exterior door.

Sash cord is broken at old double hung window.

4. ☐ **Windows.** Window problems constitute a very lengthy list: glass that is cracked, broken, loose, poorly sealed, or untempered; windows that are stuck

open, stuck shut, difficult to operate, won't lock, won't unlock, are weathered, rotted, or show signs of leakage; windows that are poorly installed, have no screens, have damage screens, have no locks, or have faulty locks. And the list goes on.

5. ☐ **Miscellaneous.** Inspection of the interior of a home should consider visible defects on all exposed surfaces, as specified in the standards of practice of the home inspection industry.

MISCELLANEOUS CHECKLIST

Having considered all of the major categories included in a home inspection, various details that do not fit within these specific subheadings remain, but they are no less important when evaluating the condition of a home. Among these are the following:

Door opens against front of wall furnace. This is a fire hazard.

1. ☐ **Cooking appliances.** Ranges, ovens, grills, microwave ovens, and venting devices should be inspected for safety, physical condition, proper installation, and operability.

Corrugated vent duct above kitchen range hood can trap grease and is therefore regarded as a fire hazard.

ASK THE INSPECTOR

Was Kitchen Vent Problem Missed by Home Inspector?

Dear Barry,

Before buying my house, I hired a home inspector to check its condition. He discovered several defects, but after closing escrow I found a problem he had missed: The exhaust hood above the kitchen range was never vented to the outside of the building. Instead, it blows smoke in my face. When I called the inspector, he said this is not a problem. How can that be? Every home I've ever owned had a range hood *that vents to the outside. Could you please clarify the legal requirements for venting a kitchen range?*

Alexis

Dear Alexis,

Outside venting of residential range hoods is an old and established practice, presumed by many to be a code requirement. But no such standard exists. The code requires exhaust hoods for commercial ranges only. Residential stoves are subject to no requirement for hoods or venting systems. Vented exhaust hoods are obviously preferable, but the lack of applicable codes prevents consumers from insisting that they be installed.

Unvented hoods, such as the one in your home, have become common because they are less costly to install than hoods that vent to the exterior, and thus, enable builders and contractors to reduce construction costs, even when obviously less desirable.

---

2. ☐ **Smoke alarms.** Smoke alarms should be evaluated to determine compliance with applicable safety standards. This includes testing each fixture to determine operability and ensuring that alarms are provided in all required locations.

Smoke alarm needs to be reinstalled.

Stair railing is required to be graspable.

3. ☐ **Staircases.** Stairs should be inspected to identify physical damage, substandard construction, and noncompliance with applicable safety standards. Numerous code requirements apply to staircase layouts, including the dimensions of treads, risers, and handrails.

4. ☐ **Insulation.** Insulation in attics, floor framing, and walls affects the efficiency of heating and cooling. In older homes, insulation typically does not meet current standards, and upgrading, although not legally required, is strongly advised.

5. ☐ **Ceiling fans.** *Casablanca*-type circulation fans are often installed by homeowners rather than by electricians. Checking the wiring in the attic often reveals substandard conditions. A common problem with such fans is the use of light dimmers for speed control, which can overheat and damage fan motors. With inexpensive fans, common defects are noisiness and wobbling.

6. ☐ **Guardrails.** Railings should be checked for compliance with applicable safety standards. In most areas, older homes are not required to comply with current standards, but upgrading is strongly advised where child safety is involved. Most significant is the 4-inch spacing limitation for openings in a safety rail system.

7. ☐ **Cabinets.** Cabinets should be inspected for damage, wear, secure attachment, operability of doors and drawers, and the condition of hardware.

8. ☐ **Miscellaneous.** The miscellaneous portion of this miscellaneous checklist could be expanded ad infinitum to include every possible apparent defect within the standards of practice of the home inspection industry. This statement is intended not merely as a point of clarification, but as a warning to those who would contact the author with complaints about particular conditions not mentioned in this homebuyer's checklist. Those who would presume such temerity shall (according to the literary protocols set forth by Samuel L. Clemens) be summarily shot.

Home inspector found seller raising fighting cocks in the basement: definitely illegal.

HOMEBUYER'S CHECKLIST

For those who would venture to field test the homebuyer's checklist presented in this chapter, here it is in its bare, naked form—unembellished, unadorned, and without benefit of the foregoing clarifications, explanations, and vociferous pontifications. Those rash spirits who would presume to apply their untrained forensic skills are advised to employ this list at their own risk.

Foundation Checklist

- [ ] Common cracks
- [ ] Large or displaced cracks
- [ ] Deterioration of foundations
- [ ] Dimensions of foundations
- [ ] Anchor bolts
- [ ] Seismic reinforcement
- [ ] Posts and piers
- [ ] Substandard repairs
- [ ] Sloped floors
- [ ] Cracked or uneven slab
- [ ] Large cracks in walls
- [ ] Misaligned doors and windows
- [ ] Inadequate ground clearance
- [ ] Additional comments

Grading and Drainage Checklist

- [ ] Ground sloped toward building
- [ ] Signs of ponding near building
- [ ] Flower beds trap water at foundation
- [ ] Evidence of past flooding below building
- [ ] Standing water below building
- [ ] Sump pumps installed
- [ ] Vapor barrier below building
- [ ] Soil erosion under or near building
- [ ] Faulty grade level at walls of building
- [ ] Raised planters against building
- [ ] Water stains on basement walls
- [ ] Additional comments

Electrical Checklist

Main Service Lines
- [ ] Underground lines
- [ ] Overhead lines
- [ ] Damaged wire insulation
- [ ] Damaged mast
- [ ] Bare connectors at the mast
- [ ] Drip loop at the mast
- [ ] Lines too close to the roof
- [ ] Lines too close to the ground
- [ ] Lines too close to a driveway
- [ ] Lines in contact with trees
- [ ] Lines too small for the service panel
- [ ] Additional comments

Breaker Panels and Fuse Panels
- [ ] Fuses or circuit breakers
- [ ] Double-tapped terminals
- [ ] Overfused circuits
- [ ] Missing handle ties at 240-volt circuits
- [ ] Damaged panel covers
- [ ] Missing panel covers
- [ ] Unprotected panel openings
- [ ] Corroded terminals
- [ ] Taped wire splices
- [ ] No main shutoff device
- [ ] Substandard service capacity
- [ ] Aluminum wiring
- [ ] Burned wires
- [ ] Faulty grounding
- [ ] Additional comments

Wiring Problems

- ☐ Knob and tube wiring
- ☐ Exposed wiring
- ☐ Substandard conduit
- ☐ Exposed wire splices
- ☐ Junction boxes without covers
- ☐ Junction boxes without wire grommets
- ☐ Exposed wire ends
- ☐ Exposed wiring in garages
- ☐ Additional comments

Outlets and Lights

- ☐ Two-prong outlets
- ☐ Ungrounded three-prong outlets
- ☐ Outlets with reversed hot and neutral
- ☐ Outlets with reversed hot and ground
- ☐ Outlets with open neutral
- ☐ Defective GFCI outlets
- ☐ Lack of GFCI protection
- ☐ Missing or damaged cover plates
- ☐ Outlets with scorch marks
- ☐ Inoperative outlets
- ☐ Electrical devices near tubs and showers
- ☐ Electrical devices without weather protection
- ☐ Attic insulation on ceiling lights
- ☐ Loose or damaged light fixtures
- ☐ Lack of essential lighting
- ☐ Lack of essential outlets
- ☐ Ceiling fans with light dimmers
- ☐ Additional comments

Plumbing Checklist

Main Water Line

- ☐ Physical damage to line
- ☐ Undersized pipe diameter
- ☐ Damaged shutoff valve
- ☐ Leaking shutoff valve
- ☐ Inaccessible shutoff valve
- ☐ Lack of a shutoff valve
- ☐ Additional comments

Water Piping within the Building

- ☐ Evidence of internal corrosion
- ☐ Restricted water flow
- ☐ Leaking at connections
- ☐ Inadequate support of pipes
- ☐ Excessive water pressure
- ☐ Copper/galvanized steel contact
- ☐ Water supply connected to drain line
- ☐ Unapproved types of water piping
- ☐ Asbestos insulation on water piping
- ☐ Additional comments

Waste Lines

- ☐ Rusted cast-iron drains
- ☐ Leaking drains
- ☐ Drains without adequate slope
- ☐ Poorly vented or unvented drains
- ☐ Clogged or restricted drains
- ☐ Inadequate support of drain pipes
- ☐ Faulty sink traps
- ☐ Additional comments

Gas or Fuel Piping

- ☐ Rusted gas piping
- ☐ Buried pipe without rust protection
- ☐ Odor of leaking gas
- ☐ Copper gas piping
- ☐ Gas connectors through construction
- ☐ Main shutoff valve at building
- ☐ Gas piping embedded in concrete
- ☐ Gas pipe unions within a building
- ☐ Protection of gas meters
- ☐ PVC plastic gas pipe
- ☐ Inadequate support of gas pipes
- ☐ Undersized gas piping
- ☐ Innumerable miscellaneous conditions
- ☐ Additional comments

Heavier-Than-Air Gas

- ☐ Propane tank near driveway
- ☐ Propane fixtures in a basement
- ☐ Overflow pan under attic furnace
- ☐ Propane gas in a fireplace
- ☐ Additional comments

Water Heaters

- ☐ Inadequate strapping or no strapping
- ☐ Raised platform in a garage
- ☐ Raised platform needs bracing
- ☐ Missing relief valve
- ☐ Missing discharge pipe
- ☐ PVC plastic discharge pipe
- ☐ Rust flakes in the burner chamber
- ☐ Rusted water connections
- ☐ Leaking water connections
- ☐ Rust damage at the casing
- ☐ Missing covers at burner chamber
- ☐ Faulty gas connections
- ☐ Faulty flue piping
- ☐ Inadequate combustion air supply
- ☐ No water shutoff valve
- ☐ Additional comments

Bathroom Plumbing
Toilets

- ☐ Loosely attached to floor
- ☐ Leaking wax seal
- ☐ Leaking tank
- ☐ Loose tank
- ☐ Doesn't flush properly
- ☐ Water runs continuously
- ☐ Flush valve leaks in tank
- ☐ Flapper leaks in tank
- ☐ Moisture damage at floor
- ☐ Floor vinyl discolored or loose
- ☐ Cracks in bowl or tank
- ☐ Loose or damaged seat
- ☐ Additional comments

Sinks, Tubs, and Showers

- ☐ Stains and discoloration
- ☐ Cracked or chipped sinks
- ☐ Corrosion on underside of sink
- ☐ Corrosion around drain openings
- ☐ Sink or cabinet not securely attached

☐ Low water volume

☐ Leaking at faucet handles

☐ Leaking at faucet base

☐ Hot and cold reversed

☐ Dripping at spout

☐ Problems with supply valves

☐ Leaking drains

☐ Congested drains

☐ Damaged drains

☐ Corroded drains

☐ Substandard drains

☐ Signs of past leakage

☐ Corroded fixtures

☐ Moisture damage

☐ Leaking shower enclosures

☐ Defective shower enclosures

☐ Leaking shower pan

☐ Lack of safety glass

☐ Room ventilation

☐ Bathroom heaters

☐ Additional comments

Kitchen Plumbing

☐ Stained or discolored sink

☐ Cracked or chipped sink

☐ Loose sink

☐ Low water volume

☐ Leaking faucet handles

☐ Leaking faucet base

☐ Faulty hand sprayer

☐ Hot and cold reversed

☐ Dripping at spout

☐ Problems with supply valves

☐ Faulty drains

☐ Substandard drains

☐ Signs of past leakage

☐ Corroded fixtures

☐ Moisture damage

☐ Loud or vibrating garbage disposal

☐ Faulty garbage disposal wiring

☐ Excessive corrosion at disposal

☐ Condition of splash guard at disposal

☐ Disposal inoperative

☐ Hazardous disposal switch location

☐ Dishwasher inoperative

☐ Dishwasher without an airgap

☐ Dishwasher makes unusual noise

☐ Dishwasher damaged

☐ Dishwasher leaks

☐ Additional comments

Laundry Plumbing

☐ Defective sink plumbing

☐ Faulty gas connections

☐ Substandard washer drain

☐ Substandard dryer vent

☐ Washer connections

☐ Additional comments

Heating Checklist

Fuel-Burning Forced-air Heat

☐ Evidence of overdue servicing

☐ Unusual noise or vibration

☐ Response to controls

☐ Intermittent performance

☐ Fire-safety clearances

☐ Damaged heat exchanger

- [ ] Flame pattern and color
- [ ] Rust flakes at burner
- [ ] Charring or soot
- [ ] Flame rollout
- [ ] Flue too close to combustibles
- [ ] Flue termination at roof
- [ ] Condition of flue cap

- [ ] Rise of flue pipe
- [ ] Damage or corrosion
- [ ] Combustion air supply
- [ ] Fuel supply
- [ ] Condition of air ducts
- [ ] Air filters
- [ ] Additional comments

Gas Heaters Other Than Forced Air

- [ ] Evidence of overdue servicing
- [ ] Unusual noise or vibration
- [ ] Response to controls
- [ ] Intermittent performance
- [ ] Fire-safety clearances
- [ ] Damaged heat exchanger
- [ ] Flame pattern and color
- [ ] Rust flakes at burner
- [ ] Charring or soot

- [ ] Flame rollout
- [ ] Flue too close to combustibles
- [ ] Flue termination at roof
- [ ] Condition of flue cap
- [ ] Rise of flue pipe
- [ ] Damage or corrosion
- [ ] Combustion air supply
- [ ] Fuel supply
- [ ] Additional comments

Hot Water Heating Systems

- [ ] Evidence of leakage
- [ ] Damage and corrosion
- [ ] High or low pressure
- [ ] High or low temperature
- [ ] Defective gauges
- [ ] Circulating pump
- [ ] Water connections
- [ ] Fuel connections
- [ ] Exhaust venting
- [ ] Combustion air supply
- [ ] Condition of radiators
- [ ] Evidence of overdue servicing
- [ ] Unusual noise or vibration
- [ ] Response to controls

- [ ] Intermittent performance
- [ ] Fire-safety clearances
- [ ] Damaged heat exchanger
- [ ] Flame pattern and color
- [ ] Rust flakes at burner
- [ ] Charring or soot
- [ ] Flame rollout
- [ ] Flue too close to combustibles
- [ ] Flue termination at roof
- [ ] Condition of flue cap
- [ ] Rise of flue pipe
- [ ] Condition of air ducts
- [ ] Air filters
- [ ] Additional comments

Electric Forced-Air Heating

- [ ] Evidence of overdue servicing
- [ ] Unusual noise or vibration
- [ ] Response to controls

- [ ] Intermittent performance
- [ ] Damage or corrosion
- [ ] Condition of air ducts

☐ Electrical shutoff near unit

☐ Air filters

☐ Additional comments

Electric Heating Other Than Forced Air

☐ Radiant ceiling heat inoperative

☐ Wall heater inoperative

☐ Wall heater damaged

☐ Wall heater improperly installed

☐ Wall heater too close to combustible material

☐ Baseboard heater inoperative

☐ Baseboard heater damaged

☐ Baseboard heater improperly installed

☐ Baseboard heater too close to combustible material

☐ Additional comments

Cooling Checklist

Air Conditioners

☐ Insufficient cooling

☐ Insufficient airflow

☐ Unit is noisy

☐ Unit vibrates

☐ Lack of condensate lines

☐ Faulty condensate lines

☐ Uninsulated refrigerant lines

☐ Faulty refrigerant lines

☐ Lack of electrical shutoff

☐ Damaged electrical shutoff

☐ Faulty electrical wiring

☐ Blocked electrical shutoff

☐ Dirty filter

☐ Lack of filter

☐ Damaged components

☐ Stable placement of unit

☐ Miscellaneous conditions

☐ Additional comments

Evaporative Coolers

☐ Insufficient cooling

☐ Insufficient airflow

☐ Unit is noisy

☐ Unit vibrates

☐ Water leakage

☐ Corrosion

☐ Physical damage

☐ Faulty fill valve

☐ Faulty supply valve

☐ Faulty water line

☐ Damaged pads

☐ Lack of electrical shutoff

☐ Damaged electrical shutoff

☐ Faulty electrical wiring

☐ Blocked electrical shutoff

☐ Dirty filter

☐ Lack of filter

☐ Damaged components

☐ Stable placement of unit

☐ Additional comments

Building Exterior Checklist

☐ Common cracks

☐ Damaged or deteriorated stucco

☐ Damaged or deteriorated masonry

☐ Damaged or deteriorated siding

- [ ] Damaged or deteriorated trim
- [ ] Moisture-damaged wood
- [ ] Weathered materials
- [ ] Deteriorated paint

- [ ] Damaged windows
- [ ] Damaged doors
- [ ] Additional comments

Yard Area Checklist

- [ ] Damaged fencing
- [ ] Defective gates
- [ ] Fencing inadequate for pool safety
- [ ] Retaining walls needed
- [ ] Retaining walls substandard
- [ ] Retaining walls damaged
- [ ] Retaining walls cracked
- [ ] Retaining walls leaning
- [ ] Common cracks in pavement
- [ ] Large cracks in pavement
- [ ] Lifted or settled pavement
- [ ] Trip hazards in pavement
- [ ] Damaged or deteriorated porches
- [ ] Damaged or deteriorated decks

- [ ] Safety rails substandard
- [ ] Safety rails damaged or deteriorated
- [ ] Stair layout substandard
- [ ] Stairs damaged or deteriorated
- [ ] Stair rails substandard
- [ ] Moisture-damaged wood
- [ ] Irrigation system inoperative
- [ ] Irrigation system damaged
- [ ] Landscaping adversely affecting building
- [ ] Tree limbs too close to roof or chimney
- [ ] Additional comments

Garage Checklist

- [ ] Damaged or deteriorated exterior
- [ ] Damaged or deteriorated roofing
- [ ] Damaged or deteriorated interior
- [ ] Interior firewall
- [ ] Interior fire door

- [ ] Garage entry door
- [ ] Automatic door opener
- [ ] Door opener safety reverse
- [ ] Additional comments

Roofing Checklist

Composition Shingles
- [ ] Damaged shingles
- [ ] Deteriorated shingles
- [ ] Substandard installation
- [ ] Too many roof layers

- [ ] Lack of underlayment
- [ ] Lack of adequate slope
- [ ] Evidence of leakage
- [ ] Additional comments

Wood Shakes or Shingles
- [ ] Damaged shakes or shingles
- [ ] Deteriorated shakes or shingles

- [ ] Substandard installation
- [ ] Too many roof layers

- [ ] Lack of underlayment
- [ ] Lack of adequate slope

- [ ] Evidence of leakage
- [ ] Additional comments

Low-Slope Roofing

- [ ] Damaged roof membrane
- [ ] Exposed roof membrane
- [ ] Deteriorated roof membrane
- [ ] Bubbled roof membrane
- [ ] Delaminated roof membrane
- [ ] Substandard installation

- [ ] Too many roof layers
- [ ] Evidence of leakage
- [ ] Sagging roof surface
- [ ] Evidence of ponding
- [ ] Additional comments

Tile Roofing

- [ ] Cracked or broken tiles
- [ ] Loose or displaced tiles
- [ ] Substandard installation

- [ ] Evidence of leakage
- [ ] Lack of required slope
- [ ] Additional comments

Metal Roofing

- [ ] Damaged metal panels
- [ ] Corroded metal panels
- [ ] Loose or lifted panels
- [ ] Loose or lifted fasteners

- [ ] Substandard installation
- [ ] Evidence of leakage
- [ ] Lack of required slope
- [ ] Additional comments

Roof Flashing

- [ ] Damaged flashing
- [ ] Corroded flashing
- [ ] Loose or lifted flashing
- [ ] Missing flashing

- [ ] Substandard installation
- [ ] Evidence of leakage
- [ ] Additional comments

Skylights

- [ ] Damaged frame
- [ ] Corroded frame
- [ ] Cracked or broken pane
- [ ] Loose or lifted skylight
- [ ] Substandard installation

- [ ] Substandard construction
- [ ] Missing or defective flashing
- [ ] Evidence of leakage
- [ ] Additional comments

Gutters and Drains

- [ ] Damaged gutters or downspouts
- [ ] Corroded gutters or downspouts
- [ ] Loose gutters or downspouts
- [ ] Missing gutters or downspouts
- [ ] System needs cleaning

- [ ] Clogged drains
- [ ] Substandard installation
- [ ] Evidence of leakage
- [ ] Additional comments

Attic Conditions

- ☐ Damaged framing
- ☐ Substandard framing
- ☐ Inadequate ventilation
- ☐ Damaged vents

- ☐ Adequate insulation
- ☐ Evidence of leakage
- ☐ Moisture damage
- ☐ Additional comments

Wood-Burning Fixtures Checklist

Masonry Fireplaces

- ☐ Damaged or deteriorated firebricks
- ☐ Cracked or loose firebricks
- ☐ Deteriorated firebrick mortar
- ☐ Substandard firebox repairs
- ☐ Substandard construction
- ☐ Damaged flue damper
- ☐ Inoperative damper
- ☐ Missing damper

- ☐ Damaged gas fixture
- ☐ Inoperative gas fixture
- ☐ Substandard gas fixture
- ☐ Inadequate clearance to combustibles
- ☐ Evidence of inadequate draw
- ☐ Evidence of rain intrusion
- ☐ Additional comments

Manufactured Fireplaces

- ☐ Damaged or deteriorated firebox liner
- ☐ Cracked or loose firebox liner
- ☐ Substandard firebox repairs
- ☐ Substandard fireplace installation
- ☐ Damaged flue damper
- ☐ Inoperative damper
- ☐ Missing damper

- ☐ Damaged gas fixture
- ☐ Inoperative gas fixture
- ☐ Substandard gas fixture
- ☐ Inadequate clearance to combustibles
- ☐ Evidence of inadequate draw
- ☐ Evidence of rain intrusion
- ☐ Additional comments

Chimney Conditions

- ☐ Damaged chimney
- ☐ Substandard chimney
- ☐ Substandard chimney repairs
- ☐ Apparent chimney settlement
- ☐ Chimney too close to combustibles
- ☐ Missing fire-stop in attic
- ☐ Chimney too short at roof
- ☐ Unlined masonry chimney
- ☐ Chimney needs cleaning

- ☐ Missing spark arrester
- ☐ Damaged spark arrester
- ☐ Substandard spark arrester
- ☐ Missing chimney cap
- ☐ Damaged chimney cap
- ☐ Substandard chimney cap
- ☐ Substandard chimney shroud
- ☐ Additional comments

Building Interior Checklist

☐ Damaged walls
☐ Damaged ceilings
☐ Damaged floors
☐ Moisture stains
☐ Moisture damage
☐ Common cracks
☐ Major cracks
☐ Substandard construction
☐ Substandard repairs
☐ Damaged windows

☐ Inoperative windows
☐ Leaking windows
☐ Damaged doors
☐ Inoperative doors
☐ Leaking doors
☐ Lack of safety glass
☐ Defective cabinets
☐ Defective countertops
☐ Additional comments

Miscellaneous Checklist

Kitchen Built-Ins

☐ Cooktop burner(s) inoperative
☐ Cooktop igniter(s) inoperative
☐ Cooktop worn/damaged
☐ Oven inoperative
☐ Oven worn/damaged

☐ Microwave oven inoperative
☐ Microwave oven worn/damaged
☐ Trash compactor inoperative
☐ Trash compactor worn/damaged
☐ Additional comments

Smoke Alarms

☐ Missing alarms
☐ Inoperative alarms
☐ Substandard alarms
☐ Misplaced alarms

☐ Damaged alarms
☐ Loose alarms
☐ Batteries needed
☐ Additional comments

Stairways

☐ Substandard stair layout
☐ Damaged stairs
☐ Substandard handrails
☐ Damaged handrails

☐ Loose handrails
☐ Missing landing
☐ Additional comments

Cabinets

☐ Substandard workmanship
☐ Damaged cabinets
☐ Damaged countertops
☐ Loose or damaged doors

☐ Loose or damaged drawers
☐ Missing or defective hardware
☐ Additional comments

ASK THE INSPECTOR

Harrowing Hazards of Home Inspection

Dear Barry,

For nearly two years, I've followed your column. In fact, it's become one of my favorite weekend features. But I'm curious: You're always visiting other people's home inspection problems and experiences. Haven't you had a few of your own? I mean, how about all the times you crawl under houses. Hasn't something happened worth relating?

Dori

Dear Dori,

Since you ask, here's the home inspection event of the week:

On the morning of Thursday last, having donned my tattered and dusty overalls—veterans of countless sojourns through the dark, uninviting recesses below a thousand homes—I raised the creaky lid of yet another dank and web-spun access hatch. But on this occasion, the sticky strands that clung to the weathered lid were not the long vacated abode of a deceased octopod. Alas, as unexpected light pierced the musty passageway, a shiny black orb scaled the stringy nest in search of darker refuge, her crimson badge declaring its icy, venomous warning.

Finding for herself a safe niche at the upper edge of the access, she secured the safety of her position while casting doubt upon mine. For I was now obliged to crawl directly beneath the dusty wooden frame to which her spiky feet deftly clung; within short inches of possible attack.

Recoiled by that chilling prospect, I found a nearby stick and searched for her, but in vain. She had found her refuge in some unseen crevice, now veiled in darkness; leaving me no option but to fulfill the perilous task for which I had been hired. Thus, with masked trepidation (for professional appearances must be maintained in the company of home inspection clients), I compressed my anxious form against the earth so as not to brush against that perilous surface as I slowly approached the subarea entry. Then, much as a child will dash for the imagined safety of bedcovers after a midnight excursion to the bathroom, I scrambled through that foreboding port.

With heart-pounding relief in the supposed security of that musty subfloor cavern, I regained my composure, assured in that breathless moment that I had passed the apex of impending danger. But then came the realization that all was not well, as my senses focused on an unwelcome stimulus: a distinct tickle on the back of my neck. My breathing stopped as the unsettling movement continued. Tense and cold with sweat, my hand took slow measured aim at the fearful prickle just above my collar. Then, with desperate suddenness, my palm struck but seemed to encounter no foreign object or wet remnant. Only the stinging receipt of that self-inflicted blow.

Had I gotten it? Was it still there? All was dark, save for the beam of my flashlight, and that provided no answer to the fearful uncertainty. I waited but felt nothing.

As long seconds became protracted minutes, I tried to focus on home inspection, straining my awareness of every sense on my alarmed skin, hoping beyond hope to be rid of that unwanted rider. But then my nerves were alerted to another fearful sensation: a prickly movement on my forearm, just beneath the sleeve of my overalls. Could it be? Oh please no! I slapped my arm furiously, as one who harbors self-directed dysfunction seeks to inflict masochistic pain. Yet I seemed to miss with every desperate stroke, and suddenly the tickle was not on my forearm but on my shoulder and then . . . my armpit!

I panicked and began to writhe—twisting and convulsing til my contorted frenzy drove the side of my head brutally against a thick wooden beam. Dazed and hyperventilated, I lay semiconscious for an indeterminate time. When my mind cleared, there was no evidence of any creeping thing, and except for the dull throbbing of my head, all seemed to be well. So I proceeded again with my inspection.

Now, what actually happened at the outset of this story was that I scurried into the crawlspace, safely skirted the spider, and inspected the crawlspace with no further mishaps. Why, you ask, the invented misadventure and the suspense of the preceding paragraphs? Well, had I been clinically honest in this report, I might have related my discovery of a leaking drain pipe, a loose electrical connection, and a small crack in the foundation. And that would have made for uninspired reading. For fanciful fabrications are frequently far funnier for friendly feature followers than factual fault-finding forays into fetid, fulsome frontiers of flea-, fly-, filth-, and fungus-infested frameworks.

And on that lighter note, we herewith adjourn these proceedings.

INDEX

Bulk Pricing Information

For special discounts on
20 or more copies of
*The Consumer Advocate's Guide
to Home Inspection,*
call Dearborn Trade Special Sales
at 800-621-9621, extension 4307,
or e-mail joseph@dearborn.com.
You'll receive great service
and top discounts.

For added visibility, please
consider our custom cover service,
which highlights your firm's name
and logo on the cover.
We are also an excellent resource
for dynamic and
knowledgeable speakers.

Dearborn™
Trade Publishing
A **Kaplan Professional** Company